LEWES&
EAST GRINSTEAD
RAILWAY
The Bluebell Line

LEWES&
EAST GRINSTEAD
RAILWAY
The Bluebell Line

Richard C. Long

Ian Allan
PUBLISHING

First published 2016

ISBN 978 0 7110 3851 6

Published by Ian Allan Publishing

an imprint of Ian Allan Publishing Ltd, Addlestone,
Surrey, KT15 2SF.

Printed in Bulgaria.

Visit the Ian Allan Publishing website at
www.ianallanpublishing.com

For Jamie and Alice

CONTENTS

Acknowledgements

My thanks are due to all those who have in any way supported or assisted me in the writing of this book. I would like to record my gratitude to the staff and volunteers of the Bluebell Railway, and in particular Roger Price of the Bluebell archives for his advice and assistance with photographic research, and Nikki Favell of the Bluebell shop, without whom I suspect this book may never have existed. I should also like to express my thanks to photographers Keith Duke, Michael Hopps, Martin Lawrence,

John Sandys and Len Walton for allowing me to make use of their excellent images throughout the book – my only regret is that space did not permit me to use more from all of them. I am grateful also to Kevin Robertson and Nick Grant of Ian Allan Publishing for their support and continued patience, even when deadlines flew past. Finally, I should like to thank my wife Gill for never once complaining about my efforts to write a book while we were in the midst of a house move.

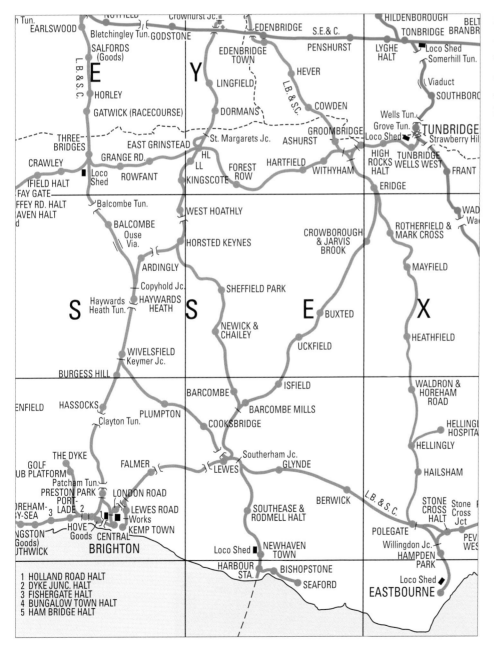

LEFT Map of the Lewes and & Grinstead Railway and associated lines in 1923 from the *British Railways Pre-Grouping Atlas and Gazetteer* **(Ian Allan Publishing Ltd).**

CHAPTER ONE

· · · · · · · · · · · · · · · · · · · ·

The origins of the Lewes & East Grinstead Railway

The Bluebell Railway of today runs over the northern half of the former Lewes & East Grinstead Railway (LEGR), which saw its first public train on 1 August 1882. Despite this relatively late appearance on the railway map, the origins of railways in the area can be traced as far back as the 'railwaymania' of the mid-19th century.

Early schemes

The earliest proposed railway in the area was in 1835, just five years after the opening of Stephenson's Liverpool & Manchester Railway, when Henry Robinson Palmer suggested routing a London to Brighton main line via East Grinstead and West Hoathly. This was just one of a number of competing route proposals for the Brighton main line, and in the end was rejected in favour of that devised by John Rennie, which received parliamentary assent in 1837 and opened through to Brighton in 1841, becoming the Brighton line that remains open to this day. This London-Brighton line was ultimately to become the backbone of the London, Brighton & South Coast Railway (LBSCR), which more than three decades later was to play a key role in the construction of the Lewes & East Grinstead Railway.

By the mid-1840s the LBSCR and its rival to the east, the South Eastern Railway (SER), were both firmly established and the area between East Grinstead and Lewes found itself on the front line between these two companies. In times of financial boom both companies would try to build lines encroaching on the other's territory, while in times of crisis both would retrench,

LEFT The Bluebell Railway of today runs over the northern half of the 1882 Lewes & East Grinstead Railway, but a proposed route between East Grinstead and West Hoathly was first suggested, as part of a London to Brighton scheme, as far back as 1835. Midway between the two settlements ex-LBSCR 'E4' Class No B473, on a down 'Golden Arrow' dining service, passes ex-SECR 'C' Class No 592 on an up train at Kingscote on 6 September 2015.
Martin Lawrence

abandoning proposed routes and, in some cases, lines that were already under construction. At this time both companies were being lobbied by residents of East Grinstead to build branches to the town from their respective lines. An SER proposal for a line from Godstone on the London-Dover line was rejected by Parliament in 1846, while an LBSCR plan for a branch from Three Bridges, which had local support, was formally approved. Unfortunately the LBSCR was now entering a period of financial crisis, to the extent that it was having to pawn its own rolling stock to stay afloat, and any notion of actually constructing the newly authorised route to East Grinstead was quickly abandoned.

Angered by being deserted by the LBSCR in this way, the residents of East Grinstead decided to form their own railway company. The East Grinstead Railway Company was created in 1852, a line to Three Bridges was authorised by Parliament the following year, and trains finally began running from Three Bridges to East Grinstead in 1855. In fact, the trains were operated by the LBSCR, which, ten years later, purchased the line it had been unwilling to construct.

East Grinstead was now firmly on the railway map, and the opening of the East Grinstead to Tunbridge Wells line would see the town's original terminus replaced with a through station in 1866. Lewes, meanwhile, had acquired its first station, providing connections to Brighton and Hastings, as long ago as 1846. The line from Lewes to Uckfield opened in 1858. However, the sparsely populated East Sussex countryside between Lewes and East Grinstead remained a transport wasteland. Roads were in poor condition, the navigable River Ouse was in decline and the railways were increasingly noticeable by their absence.

The 1860s would see a further period of boom and bust for the railways, with construction begun on two separate routes in the region that would never be completed. First, in 1864, the LBSCR obtained parliamentary authorisation to construct the Ouse Valley Railway. This was intended to leave the Brighton main line south of Balcombe Viaduct and follow the route of the Ouse Valley to a proposed station at Sheffield Park, passing north of Newick and ultimately continuing via Uckfield to Bexhill-on-Sea and terminating at St Leonards. Construction commenced between Haywards Heath and Uckfield in 1866. Meanwhile, in 1865, parliamentary approval had been given for the construction of the Surrey & Sussex Junction Railway (SSJR) north of East Grinstead. This nominally independent scheme, although supported by the LBSCR and promoted by a

ABOVE **The wax seal of the Lewes & East Grinstead Railway Company.** *Bluebell Railway Museum Archive*

number of ex-LBSCR directors, was intended to run from Croydon to Tunbridge Wells via Oxted, and construction commenced with the financial backing of the Brighton company. The SER saw this line as an encroachment by its rivals into its own territory and responded, with the cooperation of the London, Chatham & Dover Railway (LCDR), by proposing a route from London into the heart of LBCSR territory at Lewes and Brighton itself. In the event, the SER proposal never got past Parliament, while the other two schemes, the Ouse Valley Railway and the SSJR, were both to fall victim to a financial crisis triggered by the banking collapse of 1866.

In June 1866 the London-based bank of Overend & Gurney went into liquidation. It will not surprise modern-day readers that this collapse of a major bank triggered a widespread financial crisis, recession and cutbacks. In the months that followed, the LBSCR withdrew its support for the SSJR (following which the SER abandoned its own Lewes and Brighton scheme) and halted construction of the Ouse Valley Railway. Although partially constructed, neither the Ouse Valley scheme nor the SSJR would ever be completed – although parts of the route constructed for the SSJR would later be incorporated into the Oxted line. If built, the Ouse Valley Railway might have rendered the future Lewes & East Grinstead Railway redundant; instead it was to be another ten years before the prospect of a railway line through the Ouse Valley would be seriously considered. Today abandoned earthworks from both schemes remain in the Sussex countryside as a testimony to the financial crash of the 1860s.

The Lewes & East Grinstead Railway

In 1876, frustrated by the failure of earlier schemes and the continued lack of provision from the major railway companies, a group of local landowners and gentry met to promote an independent railway of their own: the Lewes, East Grinstead & London Railway Company. A meeting held at the Star Hotel, Lewes, on 30 September 1876 agreed to draw up plans for a railway between Lewes and East Grinstead and onwards towards London (in part using the abandoned route of the SSJR) as well as a branch from Horsted Keynes to join the Brighton line near Ardingly. Chaired by Henry North Holroyd, who had recently succeeded to the title of Third Earl of Sheffield, those present at the meeting consisted largely of wealthy men across whose property the line was intended to be built. Noted *The Times* in November:

LEFT Although the LEGR board did not formally cease to exist until 1884, the inclusion of the LBSCR monogram in the station architecture, as seen a century later at Kingscote, would have left contemporary passengers in no doubt as to who had actually paid for the construction of the line. *Norman Sherry, Bluebell Railway Museum Archive*

'The promoters are chiefly landowners, one of the largest of whom is Lord Sheffield, and he takes great interest in the project from the fact that he would secure railway accommodation close to his extensive estates at Fletching, Sussex.'[1]

Besides the Earl, who likely provided the bulk of the proposed funding, the committee included such influential figures as the MP for Lewes, the County Magistrate of Lewes, and the Rector of Newick. Also present at the meeting was the engineer John Wolfe Barry, who advised on the physical practicality of the scheme and was appointed to be the line's Engineer. Satisfied with Wolfe Barry's report, the meeting agreed to form an Executive Committee under the Earl of Sheffield, and to draw up plans for a Bill in the forthcoming session of Parliament.

A meeting with the LBSCR directors in October 1876 confirmed that the Brighton company was amenable towards the route south of East Grinstead and, although no financial support was offered at this stage, would not make any attempt to oppose the forthcoming Bill for a Lewes-East Grinstead line. However, the LBSCR advised against continuing with the proposed route north of East Grinstead as this could be seen as a hostile penetration into SER territory at a time when it was attempting to enter into an agreement with its old rival that would allow the Brighton company to build its own route north of the town. Initially the LEGR was happy to ignore the warnings of the LBCSR, but even the Earl of Sheffield's pockets were not bottomless. By 1877 funds for the route south of East Grinstead were running low, while the proposed route northwards, which lacked the support of either the SER or the LBSCR, was struggling to find any significant financial backing. Faced with these financial realities, the LEGR was gradually forced to become more acquiescent to the LBSCR's wishes.

The LEGR's Bill for the railway between Lewes and East Grinstead, as well as the branch to Haywards Heath, was first submitted to Parliament in February 1877, and received Royal Assent on 10 August of that year. (Included within the Act was the stipulation that a minimum service be provided of four trains per day, an apparently insignificant clause that would unexpectedly prove a major headache for the British Transport Commission when it attempted to close the line in the 1950s.) By the time of the passing of the 1877 Act the LEGR had abandoned any intention of building its own line north of East Grinstead and was heavily reliant upon the LBSCR for financial support. The new line was to be worked by the LBSCR and effectively a takeover had been agreed to. This absorption of the formerly independent company by the larger concern was to be enshrined in an Act of 1878, although the LEGR board of directors (which was now to include two LBSCR directors) would continue to meet until 1884 – by which time trains had already been running between Lewes and East Grinstead for two years. This continued existence of the LEGR board, separate from the LBSCR board, was at times to cause difficulties for both the engineer and contractor of the new line throughout the construction period, making them effectively the servants of two masters.

Construction

An example of the way the two boards of the LEGR and the LBSCR worked concurrently is seen in the appointment of the contractor, Joseph Firbank, to build the new line. Firbank was the LBSCR's choice of contractor, having already constructed a number of other lines for the company, and it was part of the takeover agreement that the LBSCR, which was effectively paying for the construction of the line, was to nominate a contractor of its own choosing. However, Firbank was technically employed by the LEGR board, on the understanding that he would take his instructions from them and from their appointed Engineer, Wolfe-Barry.

The line to be constructed between Culver Junction, north of Lewes, and East Grinstead was 17 miles 16 chains in length, and by October 1878 it was reported that Firbank was already in possession of 5 miles of the route at West Hoathly. By 19 October the first contractor's locomotive had been delivered to the site. It was at West Hoathly that the longest tunnel on the line was to be built, under the Sharpthorne Ridge, and a huge shanty town was constructed there, which at its peak included accommodation for 600 navvies and their families. Spoil removed from the 731-yard tunnel would be used in

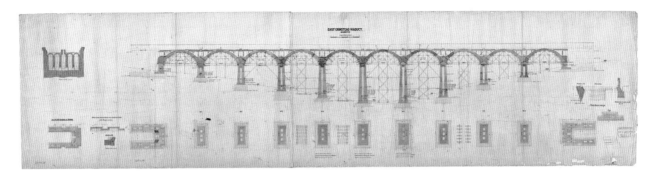

ABOVE Ex-LBSCR Class 'E4' No B473 awaits permission to proceed with a northbound train at the southern entrance to Sharpthorne Tunnel on 19 January 2013. It was at Sharpthorne that construction of the Lewes & East Grinstead Railway began in the autumn of 1878, with spoil from the tunnel excavations being used to build up earthworks elsewhere on the line. *Martin Lawrence*

ABOVE An original plan of the construction of Imberhorne Viaduct as completed up to the end of 1880. *Bluebell Railway Museum Archive*

BELOW An original 1880 construction plan for one of the shafts of Sharpthorne Tunnel. (Note the variant spelling of Sharpthorne as 'Sharp Thorn'.) *Bluebell Railway Museum Archive*

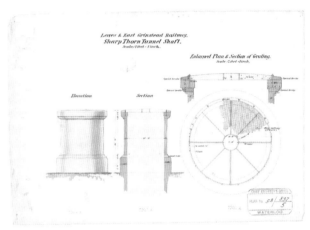

constructing earthworks elsewhere on the line, hence the need to start construction there first. Five shafts were dug from the surface to the tunnel site, three of which were later blocked, while two remained as ventilation shafts. Built slightly to the west of the alignment shown on the earliest plans, owing to opposition from local landowners, the Sharpthorne Tunnel (also known as West Hoathly Tunnel) was unfortunately built through the location of several underground springs, creating a tunnel that has forever been notoriously wet and liable to fill with dangerously large icicles in wintery conditions. The tunnel bears the date 1881, the year of its completion, above each portal.

By late 1878 work was under way at a number of locations between Horsted Keynes and East Grinstead, as well as on the branch line from Horsted Keynes to Haywards Heath, with works becoming apparent on parts of the southern section of the line by early 1879. Work on the most visually impressive construction on the line, the 10-arch Imberhorne Viaduct immediately to the south of East Grinstead, had commenced by July 1879.

Needless to say, the construction of the new railway, while largely welcomed by the local populace, did not happen without a certain level of disruption. The arrival of a large temporary workforce of navvies, estimated to be at around 2,000 men, many of them accompanied by families, in the rural Sussex countryside brought with it the usual amount of drunkenness and unruly behaviour. However, the presence of the navvies unexpectedly proved to be of great benefit during the harsh winter of 1880-81, when exceptionally heavy snowfalls in January left many outlying settlements and farmhouses cut off from the outside world. Suddenly, with all work on the line temporarily abandoned, the navvies literally became lifesavers as they set to work digging out the stranded locals with their pickaxes.

Meanwhile the damage caused by the transport of heavy construction equipment and materials over the previously lightly used local roads and tracks was of constant concern to the various local councils. Although Joseph Firbank's men attempted to carry out some repairs to the roads, this matter was later resolved, albeit not entirely, by the construction of temporary tramways between some of the work sites.

ABOVE One very tangible link between the Bluebell Railway of today and the men that constructed it more than 130 years ago is the contractor's locomotive *Sharpthorn*. Seen here on display at Horsted Keynes on 2 April 2013, the Manning Wardle 0-6-0ST, built in 1877 and named after the village that also gave its name to Sharpthorne Tunnel, was brand new when Joseph Firbank employed her on the line's construction. Last steamed in 1958, coincidentally the year of the LEGR's closure, *Sharpthorn* has been a static exhibit at the Bluebell since 1981. *John Sandys*

Obviously, as work on the line progressed the contractor's men were increasingly able to rely on locomotives and wagons to transport equipment over the completed tracks of the actual railway. By early 1881 the Imberhorne Viaduct was complete and it was possible for special parties to be conveyed in converted trucks from East Grinstead as far south as Kingscote.

The contractor

Joseph Firbank, the contractor tasked with building the LEGR, was in many ways the archetypal Victorian self-made man. Born of humble origins in 1819, by the age of seven he was working 14 hours a day in a coal mine; by the time of his death in 1886 he was High Sheriff of Monmouthshire and a rich and successful railway contractor.

Born in Bishop Auckland, County Durham, Firbank began attending night school at the age of 14, paid for out of his miner's wages. In 1840 he took the opportunity to work on the construction of a local railway, the Bishop Auckland and Weardale branch of the Stockton & Darlington Railway, and in 1841, aged only 22, he secured a sub-contract on the construction of the Woodhead Tunnel. From here his career as a railway contractor took off, undertaking larger sub-contracts and escaping the collapse of the 'railwaymania' in the mid-1840s to secure a contract under George Stephenson in 1846. In the 1850s he secured large contracts in the Monmouthshire area, which was to become his home and headquarters, and in 1859 he gained his first contract with the LBSCR. By the time he was recruited to construct the LEGR in 1877 he had become the

LBSCR's favoured contractor, having worked on a number of its lines over a period of almost two decades.

On the LEGR contract Firbank found himself answerable to two engineers, John Wolfe Barry of the LEGR and Frederick Dale Bannister of the LBSCR, as well as the two boards of the respective companies. This slightly convoluted relationship was not without its difficulties, particularly regarding the release of payments to Firbank, which were the responsibility of the LBSCR, with Wolfe Barry and the LEGR sometimes having to insist that the LBSCR settle Firbank's outstanding claims.

By 1882, while construction of the LEGR was still under way, Firbank was also jointly employed by the LBSCR and the SER on the construction of the Croydon, Oxted & East Grinstead Railway, the line north from East Grinstead that had caused the LBSCR to insist on the LEGR's abandonment of its original northern plans.

Joseph Firbank died, aged 67, in 1886. During his lifetime he had worked on such projects as the St Pancras Goods

East Grinstead Viaduct

ABOVE A 19th-century engraving showing a contractor's
locomotive on Imberhorne Viaduct during construction.
Bluebell Railway Museum Archive

Depot, the Bournemouth direct line and part of the Settle-
Carlisle line. His biography, published a year after his death in
1887, states that Firbank 'built single handed … more railways
in this country than any other contractor'[2]. Following his
death, Samuel Laing, the Chairman of the LBSCR stated,
'I believe he never skimped a bit of work in his life.'[3]

The engineers

Technically the construction of the Lewes & East Grinstead
Railway had two Chief Engineers: one appointed by the LEGR
and one appointed by the LBSCR. Needless to say, this
duplication of duties led to a certain amount of difficulty for
both men.

The Chief Engineer appointed by the LBSCR, after its
effective takeover of the LEGR, was Frederick Dale Bannister.
He was to be answerable to the LBSCR board only and
expected to oversee the work of John Wolfe Barry, the LEGR's
Engineer. As such he was expected to authorise the funding of
Wolfe Barry's work. In reality, not really being responsible for
much of the work himself, he found himself in the difficult
situation of having to defend expenditure that he himself often
had little control over.

The true Engineer of the LEGR, the man who actually
surveyed and engineered the route of the line, was John Wolfe
Barry. Having been present of the very beginning of the
company's history, at the meeting held at Lewes in September
1876, and having advised on the practicality of building a
railway between Lewes and East Grinstead, it was on the
strength of his recommendations that a decision had been
taken to proceed with a parliamentary Bill, and it was he who

had been tasked with surveying the route. Appointed as the
new company's Chief Engineer, he would subsequently,
following the LBSCR takeover, find himself in the awkward
position of being answerable to both the LEGR board and
Frederick Dale Bannister of the LBSCR. In reality, with finance
for the construction now coming from the LBSCR, and not his
employers at the LEGR, this meant that Barry would often find
himself having to chase up unsettled claims for necessary
works. (This was more due to the LBSCR board's continued
unwillingness to support the claims of an Engineer they had
not appointed than any mistrust of Wolfe Barry on the part of
Bannister.) In the event, the directors of the LEGR refused to
finally wind up their company until the LBSCR had settled
Wolfe Barry's claims to their own satisfaction in early 1884.

Despite the LBSCR's reservations, John Wolfe Barry, son of
the man who built the Houses of Parliament and friend of the
Brunel family, was a very notable Chief Engineer to have been
secured for so minor a railway. Having trained under John
Hawkshaw, designer of the stations and bridges at Charing
Cross and Cannon Street, he later worked as a consulting
engineer to the Metropolitan Railway. His official appointment
as Engineer to the LEGR took place in August 1877.
Diversifying away from railways, his most notable later work
would be the design and construction of the engineering side
of Tower Bridge, while he was also responsible for the
construction of Kew Bridge and Blackfriars railway bridge.
From 1900 to 1917 he was Chairman of Cable & Wireless.

John Wolfe Barry died in 1918, by which time he had been
elected a Fellow of the Royal Society in 1895 and President of
the Institution of Civil Engineers in 1896. He was knighted in
1897, the same year that his former sparring partner, the
LBSCR, chose to name Billinton 'B2' Class locomotive No 209
after him. His life is commemorated by a window in the nave
of Westminster Abbey, dedicated to him in 1922.

ABOVE A posed photo of the workforce at Newick & Chailey station in the latter stages of construction circa mid-1882. A contractor's locomotive stands in the up platform while the leading wagon in the down platform belongs to Stephenson, Clarke & Co, the LBSCR's coal suppliers. By 1882 delays to the construction of the stations were one of the main hold-ups to the opening of the line. *Bluebell Railway Museum Archive*

LEFT An official Board of Trade inspection train formed of three six-wheeled 1st Class saloon carriages and a four-wheeled brake vehicle pauses at Newick & Chailey station on 9 June 1882. William Stroudley, Locomotive Superintendent of the LBSCR, can be seen standing at the cab entrance of almost-new 'D' Class tank engine No 266 *Charlwood*. In fact, the LEGR failed the inspection on this day – the scaffolding present on the station platform is perhaps an indication of how much work was still to be done at this stage – and was only approved after a second successful inspection was carried out on 21 July. *Bluebell Railway Museum Archive*

Delays and inspections

In early 1882 construction was still under way and the LBSCR, having paid for the new railway, was becoming impatient to know when it might actually be in a fit state to open. By this time it appears that the route itself was largely complete and any delay was largely due to the unfinished state of the stations, upon which work had only begun the previous year, while the rather elaborate signalling arrangements on the line may also have complicated matters. (No fewer than 11 signal boxes were constructed on the 17-mile line from Culver Junction to East Grinstead.)

Another factor that had impacted on the construction of the line was the late decision taken in 1880, two years after work had begun, to construct the whole route to a double-track formation (originally the formation was to have been

double-track from East Grinstead to Horsted Keynes and single-track southwards from there.) This revision was at the suggestion of Wolfe Barry and had the backing of the LEGR board. After some debate, the LBSCR had agreed to fund the building of the double-track route, but not the actual laying of a second track. As a result, with the notable exception of

Cinder Hill Tunnel, the line was built with a double-track formation throughout from Culver Junction to East Grinstead but was laid out as a single-track railway south of Horsted Keynes, with the intention that it could be doubled at a later date if traffic levels required. In the event, the Culver Junction-Horsted Keynes section would remain a single-track route throughout its working life.

By the middle of 1882, with public complaints beginning to mount, the main factor delaying the opening of the completed LEGR was the need to pass a Board of Trade inspection. This finally occurred on 21 July 1882, following an earlier failed inspection in June. In all likelihood the failure to pass the first inspection was due in no small part to the still unfinished state of the stations at that stage. Certainly a surviving photo of the inspection train at Newick shows a station in a decidedly incomplete condition, with scaffolding standing on the still unsurfaced platforms. Thankfully, things must have improved significantly by the time of the July inspection, which the new railway passed with flying colours. On this occasion the Inspector, Colonel Yolland, was quoted in the *East Grinstead Observer* as saying that 'he had never seen work done better!'[4], no small praise indeed from the same man who had conducted the failed inspection the previous month. Almost six years had passed since the Earl of Sheffield had first chaired a meeting of interested parties at the Star Hotel in Lewes, and the Lewes & East Grinstead Railway was finally ready to take its first paying passengers!

The opening of the railway

The first train on the newly opened LEGR departed for Lewes from the Low Level platforms at East Grinstead at 6.57am on 1 August 1882. (East Grinstead station had been re-sited and reconstructed with High and Low Level platforms as part of the LEGR construction, but even at this stage, despite the successful Board of Trade inspection, the station facilities were reported to be still unfinished.) Along the route many local schoolchildren were allowed to witness the passing of the first train; a number of these would also live to see the closure of the line in the 1950s. Five trains a day were to operate in each direction on the initial timetable for the new railway. Meanwhile, the branch from Horsted Keynes to Haywards Heath was still under construction; conceived as part of the original LEGR project, it would be another 13 months before Horsted Keynes would be able to fulfil its intended role as a junction station.

BELOW Workmen and station staff pose on the platforms of the newly completed station at Horsted Keynes, apparently prior to the opening of the line. Note the break in the rails on the left-hand track (at that time the 'down' Haywards Heath line), indicating that services have yet to begin. *Bluebell Railway Museum Archive*

CHAPTER TWO

....

The Stations

A major part of the construction of the Lewes & East Grinstead Railway was the building of its characteristic and well-equipped stations. In total, six intermediate stations were constructed between the two towns, as well as a new split-level station at East Grinstead itself and a station at Ardingly on the branch to Haywards Heath (the latter will be covered in the next chapter).

All eight stations were the work of Preston-based architect Terence Harrison Myers. Rather conveniently, Myers was also the son-in-law of Frederick Bannister, the Engineer appointed by the LBSCR, and around this time was responsible for the design of a number of new LBSCR stations. All those on the LEGR were attractively designed by Myers in the so-called 'Queen Anne' style and, while the requirements of the different locations meant that no two were identical, all were built in a pleasingly uniform style that added to the character of the line. All were designed and built for the opening of the line (although not all were entirely finished on the opening day) and, although declining traffic would later lead to the demolition of various canopies, signal boxes, etc, all remained open and largely unaltered until the original closure of the line in 1955. Typically for a 19th-century rural railway, all of the intermediate stations served lightly populated areas and were mostly situated some distance from the locations they professed to serve.

Heading northwards a train would depart from the existing Lewes station (the second to serve the town, built in 1857; the station would be totally rebuilt again in 1889) and take the tracks of the Uckfield line before passing onto LEGR metals at Culver Junction.

LEFT Barcombe station is seen looking north from the road bridge shortly after the Grouping on 28 July 1923. Note the milk churns waiting on the platform. *Edward Wallis, Bluebell Railway Museum Archive*

Barcombe

1 mile 8 chains from Culver Junction, Barcombe station was the southernmost station on the LEGR and the only one to have no second platform, although ironically it was to become one of the busiest stations on the line. All passenger and staff facilities, including the station master's house, were accommodated within a single large building.

Originally planned as 'Barcombe Cross', to distinguish it from the existing Barcombe station on the nearby Uckfield line, it opened in 1882 under the name of New Barcombe. Three years later, in recognition of the fact that the LEGR station was actually closer to the village of the same name, the new station took the name Barcombe while the Uckfield line station became Barcombe Mills.

A signal box, which controlled access to a small goods yard, was originally located at the north end of the platform. This survived until 1932, when it was demolished together with most of the platform canopy.

Closed along with the rest of the line in 1955, Barcombe was unfortunately one of two stations not mentioned in the original authorising Acts, so British Railways was not legally obliged to reopen it when it was forced to reopen the line in 1956. As a result, despite being busier than most of the stations that were temporarily resurrected, Barcombe never reopened and remained out of use until the final closure of the route in 1958. The tracks were lifted in 1960, although the station building was later sold and survives to this day as a private house.

Newick & Chailey

Having passed through Cinder Hill Tunnel, which was the only structure on the single-line section of the route not built to double-track specifications, the next station was Newick

ABOVE Together with Kingscote, Barcombe station was not reopened for the 'sulky service' that operated over the Lewes to East Grinstead line during 1956-58. Here the abandoned station stands shorn of its running-in board as BR Standard Class 4MT passes with a single-coach southbound service for Lewes. *Bluebell Railway Museum Archive*

LEFT Ex-LBSCR 'E4' No 32504 enters the route of the LEGR as it climbs away from Culver Junction with the single-coach 9.30am Lewes to East Grinstead service on 11 March 1958. *Bluebell Railway Museum Archive*

RIGHT The staff pose proudly at Newick & Chailey station in 1894, only 12 years after opening. Beneath the footbridge can be seen the South signal box, while on the right stands the North box, demolished during the First World War. (This image came originally from the collection of George Piper, sometime gateman at Adversane.) *Edward Wallis*

LEFT Looking south from the footbridge at Newick & Chailey on
28 July 1923, the goods yard can be glimpsed behind the down platform
on the left while on the right the South signal box stands at the end
of the up platform. Barely 15 years later this view would have been
impossible as the up platform was taken out of use and its canopy
demolished together with the signal box and the footbridge itself.
Edward Wallis

and down platforms on either side of a passing loop, two signal boxes and substantial facilities including a refreshment room on the up platform, the station was gradually downgraded in the early decades of the 20th century. The First World War saw the closure of the refreshment room and the removal of the North signal box, while further rationalisation was to take place in the 1930s.

In 1932 the remaining signal box was removed and replaced with a ground frame on the platform, and in 1938 the loop line was downgraded to a loop siding, rendering the former up platform all but redundant. At this stage the footbridge and all of the buildings on the old up platform, including the one-time refreshment room, were demolished. The footbridge staircase on the remaining platform, being the only passenger access from the station building to the platform, was retained, meaning that the station had a decidedly unfinished appearance from that point onward.

Unlike Barcombe, Newick & Chailey was reopened together with the rest of the line in 1956, before succumbing to the final closure in 1958. Following the lifting of the tracks, the building was demolished in the 1960s and the site later infilled and built over, meaning that no trace of the former station survives today.

Sheffield Park

6 miles 30 chains from Culver Junction, the name and location of Sheffield Park station reflect the early involvement of the Earl of Sheffield in the development of the Lewes & East Grinstead Railway. Although nominally intended to serve the village of Fletching, 2 miles away, the station, described by Bluebell historian Klaus Marx as 'situated in the middle of nowhere'[5], was to all intents and purposes a de facto private station for the Earl's estate.

Originally planned by the LEGR to be named Sheffield Bridges, by the time of opening the station had officially been renamed Fletching by the LBSCR. There now followed several months of negotiation when the LEGR board at first demanded the station return to its originally proposed name before Lord Sheffield himself stepped in to announce he'd now prefer it to be Sheffield Park. The LBSCR initially offered to compromise on 'Fletching & Sheffield Park' before the Earl finally got his way and the station officially became Sheffield Park in January 1883. Even then the rejected names lingered on for many years;

ABOVE Newick & Chailey station is seen from the former up platform on 16 March 1958, the final day of operation on the Lewes to East Grinstead line. The covered staircase protruding above the canopy, once part of the footbridge, provided the only passenger access to the platform. The white stripes on the supporting columns suggest that the station has not been repainted since the wartime blackout!
Kevin Robertson collection

& Chailey, 4 miles 44 chains north of Culver Junction. Although officially opened under the name 'Newick', the station was shortly after renamed to better reflect its actual location midway between the villages of Chailey and Newick.

Unlike the other stations on the line, Newick & Chailey was located in a cutting and was accessed via a three-storey building adjacent to the down platform. The entrance was on the first floor, which was at road level, while the platforms were at basement level. Access to both platforms was via staircases at either end of a footbridge. Originally provided with both up

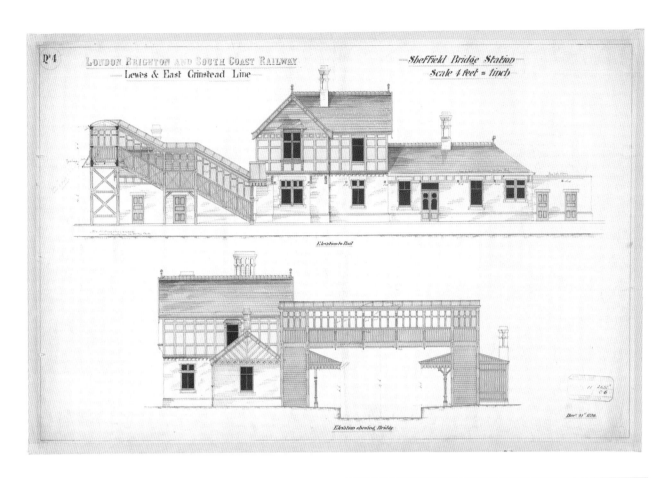

ABOVE The architect's plan, dated 21 December 1880, for Sheffield Park station. Note that at this date the station is named on the plan as 'Sheffield Bridge'. *Bluebell Railway Museum Archive*

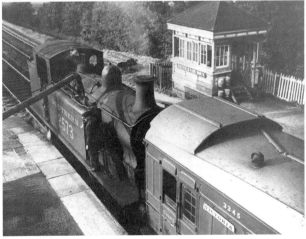

ABOVE Seen from the original footbridge, ex-LBSCR Class 'E5' tank No 2573 takes water at Sheffield Park on 25 August 1934 at the head of the 5.18pm Brighton to Victoria service. Behind it can be seen Sheffield Park North signal box, by this time downgraded to a ground frame. *Bluebell Railway Museum Archive*

'Sheffield Bridges' was written on the station's despatch bags, and 'Fletching' engraved on the original oil lamps.

Constructed with buildings on both the up and down platforms, linked by a footbridge, Sheffield Park station would see its busiest pre-preservation days in the 1880s and '90s when the Earl of Sheffield played host to a number of cricket matches, military displays and Royal visits. On several

ABOVE LEFT This posed Victorian photo shows the original main Sheffield Park signal box, which stood at the south end of the up platform. In 1934 both signal boxes were taken out of use and replaced by an open frame on the down platform. *Bluebell Railway Museum Archive*

TOP The main station building at Sheffield Park, little changed since Victorian days, is seen a few days before closure on 8 March 1958. Note that the 'Entrance to Station' sign on the extreme left points away from the porch, a reminder that the once-busy station was unstaffed by this time. A sign on the porch itself advertises the presence of a telephone, and the postbox is visible within. No doubt the wordy posters on the wall are announcing the forthcoming closure of the line. Only 2½ years later the station would be reopened by the new Bluebell Railway. *Denis Cullum, Bluebell Railway Museum Archive*

ABOVE At a casual glance the current signal box on Sheffield Park's Platform 1 appears to be an original feature of the Victorian station, but in truth it dates only from the early days of preservation. Following preservation, the open frame on the down platform attracted a level of attention from onlookers that was deemed to be unsafe, so the current structure, seen here on 26 July 2014, was hastily constructed around the existing frame during the winter of 1961/62. *Keith Duke*

ABOVE Viewed in December 2015, the Victorian porch at Sheffield Park displays the stained glass windows that were restored during 2015, the original panes having been removed during the Southern Railway era. *John Sandys*

ABOVE Sheffield Park station continues to exude a pre-Grouping atmosphere as 1905-built SECR 'H' Class 0-4-4T No 263 stands at the north end of the former down platform at the head of an East Grinstead train on 6 June 2016. *Martin Lawrence*

occasions the Earl's estate would be used as the venue for the visiting Australian cricket team to play their opening match on English soil – often playing against teams captained by W. G. Grace. Thousands would arrive by train to witness these matches, often including the Prince of Wales, the future King Edward VII, himself a personal friend of the Earl. Sadly, these glory days could not last forever and the inevitable decline in Sheffield Park's fortunes set in following the death of the Earl in 1909, and the subsequent outbreak of the First World War in 1914.

Originally provided with two signal boxes, the North signal box was later downgraded to a shunting cabin before both were abolished and replaced with a ground frame on the down platform. The original station footbridge was subsequently removed circa 1949.

Following the final BR closure in 1958, Sheffield Park received a new lease of life in 1960 when it became the first station acquired and reopened by the newly formed Bluebell Railway Preservation Society. Initially held on a five-year lease, together with the railway towards Horsted Keynes (Bluebell trains were not permitted access to Horsted Keynes station itself until late

1961), the station was purchased outright in 1968 and has now served as the headquarters and southern terminus of the Bluebell Railway for more than five decades. During this period the station buildings have been sensitively restored to original LBSCR condition (one of the most recent projects being the restoration of the stained glass windows in the station porch), while a host of new buildings have been constructed to serve the needs of a major preserved railway. 1986 saw the opening of a replacement ex-LBSCR footbridge, acquired from Lingfield station in 1985, as well as the opening of a major new buffet building. Designed to harmonise with the existing buildings, the latter has since been extended twice and now also contains administrative offices and the station shop.

Other facilities constructed around the station over the past five decades include extensive locomotive works and carriage sheds and an adjoining museum.

Horsted Keynes

At 10 miles 68 chains north of Culver Junction can be found the largest intermediate station on the LEGR. On the face of it Horsted Keynes has always been something of an oddity – a large interchange station in the midst of the rural Sussex countryside. Serving a village situated about 1½ miles away and with a population recorded in the 1881 census of only 811 inhabitants, Horsted Keynes was nonetheless the junction where the branch to Ardingly and Haywards Heath departed

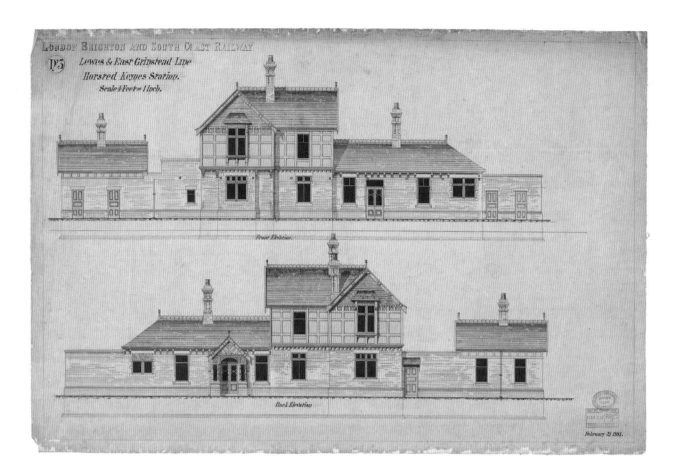

LONDON BRIGHTON AND SOUTH COAST RAILWAY
N°5 *Lewes & East Grinstead Line*
Horsted Keynes Station.
Scale 4 Feet = 1 Inch.

Front Elevation.

Back Elevation.

February 21 1881.

ABOVE An architect's plan, dated 21 February 1881, for the front and back elevations of the main station building at Horsted Keynes. *Bluebell Railway Museum Archive*

RIGHT During the years 1905-09 the little-used carriage sidings at Horsted Keynes became a temporary locomotive store for the LBSCR, with sometimes more than 30 engines to be found there awaiting either repair or scrap. This line-up at Horsted Keynes is undated, but as the leading locomotive, 'D1' Class 0-4-2T No 4 *Mickleham*, was withdrawn in 1907, this may well have been its last resting place before being broken up. *Bluebell Railway Museum Archive*

from the main LEGR route, and as such was generously provided for. (Indeed, Horsted Keynes was originally signalled on the assumption that the double-track East Grinstead to Haywards Heath route was the main line, with the single line south to Lewes being treated as the branch.)

As built, the station had five platform faces, linked by a subway, facing onto four running lines (the down line to Lewes was, unusually, faced by platforms on both sides) with buildings and canopies on all platforms. Two refreshment rooms were provided and, like several other stations on the route, signal boxes could be found at both the north and south ends. The size of the station was largely a result of the fact that it was hoped that the line from Haywards Heath to East Grinstead via Horsted

Keynes would become a major relief route for Brighton to London trains, although in the event much of this traffic failed to materialise and, like the rest of the route, facilities were gradually reduced as time went by. Rationalisation in 1914 saw the track layout revised, with the former up main Haywards Heath line becoming a siding and the North signal box being downgraded to a shunting frame. To facilitate this all of the buildings on the furthermost island platform, including the canopy, were demolished to give the signalman in the South box a clear view of the north end of the station. Further rationalisation followed in 1935, when the station became an unlikely outpost of the third-rail Southern Electric network; the Ardingly branch was electrified largely to avoid Seaford services

ABOVE Preserved 'Terrier' No 72 *Fenchurch* passes the surviving South signal box at Horsted Keynes as it runs round its train prior to returning to Sheffield Park on a wintery 29 November 1969. *Len Walton*

BELOW The driver of 2-BIL unit No 2039 hands over the staff for the Ardingly branch as his train enters Horsted Keynes on 20 May 1961. It seems hard to imagine now, but electric trains were a daily sight at Horsted Keynes station between the years 1935 and 1963. *J. H. W. Kent, Bluebell Railway Museum Archive*

ABOVE Passengers join a Bluebell Railway service to Sheffield Park at the temporary Horsted Keynes (Bluebell Halt) station on 15 June 1961. 'P' Class No 323 *Bluebell* is at the rear of the 'Chesham set' carriages, while another locomotive will be at the front – the lack of run-round facilities at the halt meant that all Bluebell trains had to be top-and-tailed at this stage. *Fox Photos, Bluebell Railway Museum Archive*

having to reverse at Haywards Heath. One upshot of this was that Horsted Keynes was now provided with electric lighting, the only intermediate station between East Grinstead and Lewes not to remain lit by oil lamps until closure.

A generous provision of sidings at Horsted Keynes, originally used to hold special trains on the occasion of gala events at Sheffield Park, meant that the station was often used to store unusual items of rolling stock. Between 1905 and 1909, while Brighton Works was being rebuilt, a large number of elderly LBSCR locos, some partially dismantled, were stored in the sidings awaiting repair or scrapping. During the Second World War the isolated nature of the location meant that the sidings were again utilised, this time to store both unused passenger stock and trainloads of military equipment away from prying eyes and bombs falling on the cities. At this time it was not unusual to see Pullman cars and electric units berthed alongside ammunition trains and ships' propellers.

The continued existence of the electrified line to Haywards Heath meant that Horsted Keynes station was not closed with the rest of the Lewes to East Grinstead route in 1958. Unfortunately the fact that only one platform face had ever been electrified meant that, even after the other platforms had

ABOVE SECR 'C' Class No 592 makes an impressive northbound departure from Platform 2 at Horsted Keynes on 14 April 2012, a far cry from the days when this platform was the sole preserve of electric units for the Ardingly branch. The canopy over Platforms 1 and 2, demolished during the First World War, was rebuilt by the Bluebell in 1999 and now appears indistinguishable from the surviving canopy on Platforms 3 and 4. BR Standard Class 9F No 92240 stands in Platform 1, while the sidings to the right are once again being used for rolling stock storage. *Keith Duke*

been made redundant, passengers for Ardingly and Haywards Heath were still forced to use an island platform that lacked any waiting facilities or canopy before exiting the station via the subway.

In 1960 the Bluebell Railway started operating a steam service from Sheffield Park. Initially Bluebell trains were not permitted access to the still BR[6]-owned Horsted Keynes station, having instead to terminate at a temporary 'Horsted Keynes (Bluebell Halt)' located on the other side of the road bridge from the main station. The need for the halt was to be short-lived for on the final day of the 1961 running season, 29 October, the Bluebell was at last permitted to run a passenger service into the main station, meaning that for the first time direct passenger interchange was possible between BR electric and Bluebell steam services. This convenience was unfortunately not enough to save the Ardingly branch from closure and it would be a mere 24 months later that the last electric service would run into Horsted Keynes station.

Together with Sheffield Park, Horsted Keynes station was purchased outright by the Bluebell Railway in 1968. Serving for many years as the northern terminus of the preserved line, the station has been restored to Southern Railway condition – albeit with the buildings and canopies demolished by the LBSCR in the First World War reinstated on Platforms 1 and 2 in 1999. The site also houses the Bluebell's Carriage & Wagon Department, a carriage works viewing gallery being accessible from Platform 5.

West Hoathly

Situated immediately to the north of the 731-yard-long Sharpthorne Tunnel, West Hoathly was 13 miles 13 chains from Culver Junction and, like most intermediate stations on the LEGR, was about a mile from the village of the same name. Being on the double-track section of the line, the station was provided with two platforms linked by a covered footbridge and was arguably not dissimilar in appearance to Sheffield

Park. The entrance to the station was via a two-storey building on the up platform, which included the station master's house, while a canopy and wooden waiting shelter stood on the down platform. A single signal box, which survived in use until 1955, was situated at the north end of the down platform.

The station closed for the final time, together with the rest of the line, in 1958. The double-track section from Horsted Keynes to East Grinstead, initially mothballed by BR, was formally closed to all traffic in 1963, and in 1964 the footbridge and down-side buildings at West Hoathly were demolished by the contractors engaged to lift the tracks. The main station building was demolished in 1967 when the whole site was cleared for housing development. However, this did not proceed straight away and eight years later, in 1975, the Bluebell took advantage of an opportunity to purchase the site of the station as the first step of a long-term plan to extend the preserved railway northwards towards East Grinstead.

BELOW A panoramic view of West Hoathly looking south on 30 April 1955, one month before the first closure of the line. At the northern end of the station can be seen the signal box at the end of the down platform and the cattle dock at the end of the up platform. The looming entrance to Sharpthorne Tunnel can be glimpsed at the southern end of the station. *Bluebell Railway Museum Archive*

ABOVE Viewed from the top of Sharpthorne Tunnel, the remains of the platforms are still visible as Peppercorn 'A1' 'Pacific' No 60163 *Tornado* passes the site of the long-demolished West Hoathly station on 10 September 2013. The train is the 'Cathedrals Express', the first steam-hauled London departure to travel over the northern half of the Bluebell line since 1959. *Len Walton*

LEFT This undated BR-era shot of West Hoathly shows the two-storey station house on the up platform and the covered footbridge linking the platforms, all of which survived until after the closure of the line. *Bluebell Railway Museum Archive*

BELOW LEFT The exterior of Kingscote station is seen one day before closure on 27 May 1955, showing the so-called 'Queen Anne' style that was so typical of all the LEGR stations. *Denis Cullum, Bluebell Railway Museum Archive*

It would be a very long time before trains returned to West Hoathly, but in 1992 the site became the temporary northern terminus of the Bluebell Railway. A run-round loop was built, but this was removed two years later when trains began running through to Kingscote. No platforms were provided and passengers were not permitted to alight from trains at this temporary terminus.

To date, a combination of planning restrictions, local uncertainty and financial demands have prevented the Bluebell Railway from constructing a new station at West Hoathly, but its reinstatement remains one of the railway's long-term ambitions.

Kingscote

If all of the intermediate stations on the LEGR served sparsely populated areas, it was perhaps Kingscote, one of the quietest stations on the entire LBSCR network, whose remoteness drew particular comment. 15 miles 1 chain north of Culver Junction, it was described in a guide book of 1887 as 'A railway station without a village'[7]. In 1954, with the entire line facing imminent closure, R. C. Riley wrote that '[the station] is almost entirely devoid of both passenger and freight traffic, and its continued existence for so many years is surprising. It serves a few houses in almost exclusively rural surroundings.'[8]

A two-platform station, with the main two-storey building on the up platform, Kingscote originally had canopies and buildings on both platforms (the down platform buildings, but not the canopy, were removed in Southern Railway days) and shared with Horsted Keynes the distinction of having a subway instead of a footbridge. A signal box was located at the north end of Platform 2.

RIGHT The 'new' signal box at Kingscote, constructed in 1996 but not commissioned until February 2016, is seen here on 20 January 2016. The box incorporates the cabin from the former Brighton Upper Goods signal box. *Martin Lawrence*

BELOW A decade after the last passenger service called at Kingscote, the station appears remarkably unchanged on 23 January 1965. The former up platform is strewn with sleepers from the recently lifted up line, while the down line awaits lifting. *E. Wilmshurst, Bluebell Railway Museum Archive*

Closed with the rest of the line in 1955, Kingscote, like Barcombe, was not named in the original Act of 1877, so was not reopened when the line was reprieved in 1956. The signal box was demolished when the tracks were taken up in 1964, but the surviving station buildings had been purchased privately for residential use and so escaped the attentions of the contractors.

In 1985 Kingscote began a new chapter in its existence when, having been placed on the market in the previous year, it was successfully purchased by the Bluebell Railway as part of its ongoing extension plans. By this time the down platform had been demolished and the main building on the up platform was in a sorry state of repair following a number of ill-judged and half-finished alterations. Work commenced immediately to end the building's decline and restore it to its former condition.

Trains returned to Kingscote in 1994 and from then until 2013 it took on arguably the most important role in its existence, serving as the northern terminus of the Bluebell Railway, with passengers arriving by bus from East Grinstead station. By this time the station had been fully restored, many missing fixtures and fittings being replaced with parts rescued from stations elsewhere on the LBSCR system, and the down platform, including canopy, had been completely rebuilt. (Ironically, the original down platform canopy had been removed by Bluebell volunteers in the 1970s, at the request of the then owner.) A replacement signal box, utilising the redundant cabin from the former Brighton Upper Goods, was constructed in 1996 although

ABOVE This atmospheric undated shot of East Grinstead Low Level platforms was probably taken in the 1950s. The two children stand on Platform 1, perhaps awaiting a train to Lewes, while the overbridge carries the four High Level platforms, swept away following the closure of the Three Bridges to Tunbridge Wells route in the 1960s. The much-altered Low Level platforms survive today as the terminus of the electrified route from London. *Norman Sherry, Bluebell Railway Museum Archive*

not brought into use until early 2016. (Train movements for the intervening two decades were controlled by a 'temporary' cabin located three-eighths of a mile to the south of the station.)

East Grinstead

Having crossed Imberhorne Viaduct, trains from Lewes entered a split-level station at East Grinstead, 17 miles 16 chains from Culver Junction. Constructed to the design of Thomas Myers, this was the third East Grinstead station, having been purpose-built to facilitate interchange between the LEGR and the existing lines already serving the town. As such, it was constructed in the same 'Queen Anne' architectural style as the rest of the LEGR stations, despite its unusual layout.

The earliest East Grinstead station had opened as far back as 1855, as the terminus of the line from Three Bridges, and was replaced in 1866 by a new through station, on a different site, when the line from East Grinstead to Tunbridge Wells opened. (The, much altered, main building from the 1855 station survives today and is located near the

BELOW This posed postcard view from the turn of the last century shows the exterior of East Grinstead station. This was the third station to serve the town, constructed in 1882-83 for the opening of the LEGR and, although altered beyond recognition over the past five decades, is technically still the same National Rail station that exists today. *Bluebell Railway Museum Archive*

S 5289   L. B. & S. C. RAILWAY STATION. EAST GRINSTEAD

aptly named Beeching Way.) The 1866 station proved short-lived and was itself superseded by the construction of the LEGR station 300 yards to the west in 1882-83.

Constructed at right angles to one another, the Low Level station at East Grinstead had two platforms while the High Level station, consisting of two island platforms, had four platform faces. The High Level platforms served the Three Bridges to Tunbridge Wells route while the Low Level platforms served the LEGR route as well as, from 1884, trains to London via Oxted. Half a mile to the north of the Low Level station was St Margaret's Junction, allowing trains from London to gain access to either the Low or High Level platforms, allowing rail interchange between the different routes.

The main station building faced onto the Low Level platforms, although the High Level platforms were also provided with refreshment rooms. Both High Level island platforms could be reached by staircases from either Low Level platform, while a passenger footbridge also linked the Low Level platforms. Like many stations on the LEGR route, the Low Level station originally had signal boxes to the north and south, but the North box was taken out of use in the 1920s. The South box survived in use until as recently as 1987, long after the High Level station had ceased to exist.

Following the initial closure of the East Grinstead to Lewes route in 1955, most London-bound services were re-routed into the High Level station, via St Margaret's Junction, and the Low Level station fell gradually into disuse. This situation was later reversed when the Three Bridges to Tunbridge Wells line fell victim to the cuts of Dr Richard Beeching (himself a local resident) in the 1960s. The last passenger train served the High Level station in January 1967 and from then on all London services, now the only remaining route into the town, used the Low Level platforms.

By 1971 the High Level station had been demolished and almost all trace of the 1882 LEGR station on the Low Level platforms had been swept away. The station has undergone further rebuilds since and is unrecognisable from that which existed from the 1880s to the 1960s. Despite this, the two platforms that constitute the Network Rail East Grinstead station of today are still, technically, the Low Level platforms laid out by Thomas Myers in 1882.

In 2009 construction work began on a new platform, to the south of the existing site, to serve Bluebell Railway trains, and March 2013 saw the first timetabled Bluebell passenger service pull into the station, marking the return of steam trains to East Grinstead for the first time since the 1960s. The physical connection to the Network Rail network means that, for the first time since the tracks were lifted in 1964, trains are once again able to run through from London and elsewhere and continue southward onto LEGR metals.

ABOVE Ex-SECR 'P' Class No 323 *Bluebell* prepares to depart from the new Bluebell Railway station at East Grinstead with the 1913-built LNWR Observation Car for an 'Autumn Tints' special on 9 October 2015. The platform buildings on the left, which include disabled facilities, were opened by the Mayor of East Grinstead in August 2015. *Martin Lawrence*

CHAPTER THREE

....

The Ardingly branch and the route to London

As conceived in 1876, the original LEGR scheme was to include a branch from

Horsted Keynes to connect with the main London-Brighton line at Haywards Heath,

and a route north of East Grinstead towards London. In the event the branch opened

in 1883, just one year later than the main Lewes to East Grinstead line, while the line

towards London was abandoned in the face of LBSCR opposition, only to be replaced

by the LBSCR's own northwards route, which opened from East Grinstead to Oxted in

1884. In conjunction with the double-track line between East Grinstead and Horsted

Keynes, these two lines would allow the northern section of the LEGR to form

a diversionary route for traffic on the London-Brighton line.

Ardingly Station, L. B. & S. C. Railway.

LEFT In this undated, possibly Edwardian, postcard image of Ardingly station in LBSCR days, a 'D' Class tank engine prepares to depart from the down platform with a goods service towards Haywards Heath. *Bluebell Railway Museum Archive*

The Ardingly branch

The branch to Haywards Heath ran via Ardingly and connected with the Brighton line at Copyhold Junction, to the south of the Ouse Valley Viaduct. It was conceived and authorised as part of the original Lewes & East Grinstead Railway, and as such was surveyed and engineered by John Wolfe Barry. Construction by Joseph Firbank's men commenced at around the same time as works elsewhere on the LEGR. Indeed, priority was given to the completion of the branch, which was intended to open at the same time as the rest of the LEGR, although construction delays meant that the opening actually took place on 3 September 1883, some 13 months after passenger services had begun operation between Lewes and East Grinstead.

The 4-mile branch to Copyhold Junction had only one station, at Ardingly (a second station, at Lyewood, was also authorised but never constructed), and two major engineering features, the 218-yard Lyewood Tunnel and the five-arch, 117-yard Sheriff Mill Viaduct. The latter structure, which sadly no longer exists, was crossed by Haywards Heath-bound trains as they curved away

ABOVE At Copyhold Junction in the early 20th century, LBSCR 'B1' Class 0-4-2 No 193 hauls a rake of six-wheelers off the Ardingly branch towards Haywards Heath. *M. Bennett, Bluebell Railway Museum Archive*

RIGHT The signal box at Copyhold Junction, where the Ardingly branch joined the Brighton line, was built in 1912 but only survived in use until 1932. *Edward Wallis*

BELOW The junction layout at the south of Horsted Keynes station is seen on 8 March 1958. The route towards Lewes, just days away from closure, turns away to the left of the picture while the Ardingly branch, itself only secure for another five years, veers off to the right.

Pamlin Prints, Bluebell Railway Museum Archive

LEFT Another pre-Grouping postcard view of Ardingly station, this time showing the T. H. Myers-designed station house, which stood at a right angle to the platforms below. *Bluebell Railway Museum Archive*

BELOW An unusual view of Ardingly station, seen looking west from beneath the road bridge. The down platform is in the centre of the image and the footbridge continues to the left as the only link to the station house, situated away from the platforms at road level. The running-in board reads 'Ardingly for Ardingly College'. *Bluebell Railway Museum Archive*

from the Lewes line after departing from Horsted Keynes. The branch was double-tracked throughout and provided with a signal cabin at Ardingly station. A signal box was also constructed at Copyhold Junction in 1912 (originally branch trains had continued from Copyhold to Haywards Heath on separate tracks parallel to the main line), but was decommissioned in 1932 when Haywards Heath was rebuilt and resignalled with colour lights prior to forthcoming electrification.

Ardingly station

Located 2 miles 22 chains from Horsted Keynes, Ardingly was designed by T. H. Myers in the same architectural style as that employed for the stations between Lewes and East Grinstead. However, it differed from the others in having the station house located at road level and at right angles to the down (westbound) platform. The road itself crossed the railway by a brick arch immediately east of the station. Access to the two platforms, which were at a lower level, was via a long corridor that effectively formed a continuation of the covered station footbridge. Besides the footbridge, both platforms had covered awnings, and a basic waiting room, open to the elements, was provided on the down platform. A small signal box stood on the down platform at the western end. The station remained largely unchanged throughout its working life although, as at Horsted Keynes, electrification of the branch in the 1930s brought the installation of electric lighting to replace the original oil lamps.

As with many stations on the LEGR, a sparse local population failed to provide much passenger traffic although the station was initially kept busy with goods traffic, much of it agricultural. The one exception to this was traffic generated by the local public school, Ardingly College, the proximity of which was acknowledged by the designation 'Ardingly for Ardingly College' on the station's running-in boards. At the beginning and end of each term the station would briefly

ABOVE This undated photo shows Ardingly signal box, which stood at the western end of the down platform. *Lens of Sutton, Bluebell Railway Museum Archive*

become a hive of activity with special trains laid on for the transport of up to 250 pupils and their accompanying luggage to and from the school.

The school was honoured by the Southern Railway in 1933 when newly built 'Schools' Class locomotive No 917 visited the station to receive the name Ardingly.

Electrification

The branch received an unexpected investment in 1935 when it was included in the Southern Railway's extension of the third-rail network to Lewes, Seaford, Eastbourne and Hastings. In truth the electrification to Horsted Keynes was almost certainly included simply to avoid the necessity of Seaford line trains reversing at Haywards Heath, where spare platform space was limited. Certainly it is unlikely that the traffic generated by the combined population of Horsted Keynes and Ardingly could ever have justified the electrification of the branch in itself. Electric trains started running on this latest phase of the Southern's electrification programme on Sunday 7 July 1935 – except for the Ardingly branch, which, due to local opposition, had never had a local Sunday service and on which the first electric passenger service began a day later, on the Monday. (The ban on Sunday trains was finally lifted in 1945.) Electric services were normally handled by 2-NOL units and later, under BR ownership, by either 2-BIL or 2-HAL units.

Another consideration in electrifying the line from Haywards Heath to Horsted Keynes was the prospect of one day extending the third rail from Horsted Keynes to East Grinstead, and onward toward London – thereby finally realising the full potential of the branch as part of a diversionary route for the Brighton main line. Such a scheme was first seriously considered by the Southern Railway in 1939 before being waylaid by the outbreak of the Second World War. The idea was revived again in the final days of the Southern Railway, and on further occasions under British Railways' ownership, but the potential benefits were ultimately not enough to save the branch from closure.

BELOW Electrification came to the Ardingly branch in 1935. In this view from 9 September 1962, 2-BIL unit No 2063 prepares to depart from the down platform. '37' was the regular headcode for the Seaford-Horsted Keynes route. *J. H. Aston, Bluebell Railway Museum Archive*

ABOVE 2-NOL unit No 1849 stands at the solitary electrified platform at Horsted Keynes with an Ardingly line service on 15 March 1958. If the Southern Railway's pre-war expansion plans had been realised, the third-rail network could have continued northward from here to East Grinstead. *L. W. Rowe, Bluebell Railway Museum Archive*

ABOVE 2-BIL unit No 2149 leaves Lywood Tunnel with a Horsted Keynes to Seaford service in May 1959. *S. C. Nash, Bluebell Railway Museum Archive*

Closure

In 1954, with the Lewes to East Grinstead line already slated for closure, an article in *The Railway Magazine* was able to definitely state of the Ardingly branch that 'It is not the intention of the British Transport Commission to close this branch.'[9] Yet in truth the branch was living on borrowed time, and in 1963 it received the dubious distinction of becoming the first outpost of the Southern Electric network to be axed. With the benefit of hindsight it seems remarkable that the branch to Horsted Keynes could ever have been expected to survive once the prospect of onwards travel towards other, more significant, destinations had been extinguished with the closure of the Lewes to East Grinstead line.

BELOW In January 1959 the line between Ardingly and Horsted Keynes was singled and the former down line converted into a siding that, for the next six months, was used to store a 2-mile line of brand-new units intended for the Kent Coast electrification scheme. 4-CEP unit No 7119 stands adjacent to the former Ardingly down distant signal post in this image from 9 May 1959. On the far right the new down distant signal guards the newly singled former up line. *Bluebell Railway Museum Archive*

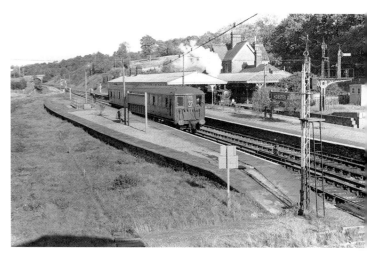

ABOVE The final working over the Ardingly branch, before tracklifting commenced, took place on 13 May 1964 when the Bluebell Railway took delivery of 'A1X' 'Terrier' Class No 32636 (better known as No 672 *Fenchurch*) and ex-LBSCR van No 270. In this view, *Fenchurch* propels the van over the seldom-photographed Sheriff Mill Viaduct. *K. D. Chown, Bluebell Railway Museum Archive*

LEFT By 30 August 1959, when this photo of BSK No 3672 of set No 951 was taken, the electric units had entered service on the Kent Coast and their place on the Ardingly branch had been taken by the redundant steam-hauled stock they had displaced. Two years later, in October 1961, it was recorded that more than 130 condemned coaches were stored between Ardingly and Horsted Keynes. *J. J. Smith, Bluebell Railway Museum Archive*

Services between Lewes and East Grinstead ceased for the final time in 1958 but – since only one track at Horsted Keynes had ever been electrified – passengers for the branch still continued to brave the elements on the canopy-less furthermost platform at the large and otherwise built-up station.

The run-down of the branch arguably began as early as 1959 when the Ardingly-Horsted Keynes section was singled and the former down line used to store stock destined for –

LEFT Even the attraction of a direct connection with the new Bluebell Railway proved unable to rescue the flagging fortunes of the Ardingly branch. 2-BIL No 2115 departs from the sole electrified platform at Horsted Keynes with the 2.16pm Seaford service on 27 October 1962, while behind it stands 'E4' No 473 *Birch Grove* with the 2.20pm train for Sheffield Park. Exactly 12 months later the branch saw its final passenger service. *S. C. Nash, Bluebell Railway Museum Archive*

RIGHT The eastern half of the Ardingly branch, between Ardingly and Horsted Keynes, was lifted between 15 July and 21 September 1964, with Bluebell steam engines hired in to work the contractors' trains. In this undated view the third rail has already been lifted and the trackbed is looking decidedly overgrown as ex-LBSCR 'E4' Class No 473 *Birch Grove* approaches Lywood Tunnel with a demolition train. *Klaus Marx, Bluebell Railway Museum Archive*

and subsequently stock made redundant by – the Kent Coast electrification. The first Bluebell Railway service arrived at the temporary Horsted Keynes (Bluebell Halt) station in 1960 and from 1962 the two railways regularly shared the main station, providing direct interchange, via the subway, between electric and Bluebell steam services for the first time. Yet even the attraction of the Bluebell Railway, as well as the continued possibility of extending the electric service northwards via the mothballed Horsted Keynes to East Grinstead line, was not enough to reverse the fortunes of the Ardingly branch and the final passenger service ran on the 27 October 1963.

The very last train to traverse the line, other than those of the demolition contractors, was on 13 May 1964 when ex-LBSCR 'Terrier' locomotive *Fenchurch* was delivered to the Bluebell Railway under its own steam. (The first such working had occurred in 1960 when the Bluebell's first ever items of rolling stock, the 'Terrier' *Stepney* and two coaches, had arrived via the branch, and from then until 1964 this was the usual route for new Bluebell stock to arrive.)

After closure the western section of the branch, from Copyhold Junction to Ardingly, was singled and retained to act as a siding to the aggregates depot that had been established there by Amey Roadstone on the site of the old goods sidings. The track east from Ardingly to Horsted Keynes was lifted shortly after and Sheriff Mill Viaduct was demolished in 1968, severing the route to Horsted Keynes.

RIGHT On 3 September 1983 the Bluebell Railway celebrated the centenary of the Ardingly branch (or at least what was left of it) with the operation of the first passenger train in two decades over the surviving stub from Haywards Heath to Ardingly. British Rail DMU No L582, pictured here at Copyhold Junction, was hired for the occasion and operated a series of shuttle trips up and down the normally freight-only line. *P. Barnes, Bluebell Railway Museum Archive*

The Ardingly branch today

Today much of the route of the Ardingly branch survives. The aggregates plant still exists at Ardingly, occupying the site of the former platforms as well as the sidings, and is still served by regular freight trains from Copyhold Junction. The roadside station house survives in remarkably good condition and serves as office accommodation for Hanson, which now owns the depot. The trackbed east from Ardingly to Horsted Keynes is now in the ownership of the Bluebell Railway, which has a

ABOVE LEFT Lywood Tunnel, seen here in April 1997, perhaps awaits the day when trains will return. *Jim Turtle, Bluebell Railway Museum Archive*

ABOVE RIGHT This view from the former High Level platforms at East Grinstead shows the line towards London opened by the LBSCR in 1884 after the proposed LEGR route north was abandoned in 1877. *Lens of Sutton, Bluebell Railway Museum Archive*

BELOW Maunsell 'U1' Class No 31900 departs from West Hoathly with the northbound 3.28pm Haywards Heath to London Bridge service on 7 May 1955. Although London-bound services continued to run via the Ardingly branch and over the northern section of the LEGR until the late 1950s, the full potential of the route was arguably never fully realised. *Bluebell Railway Museum Archiv*

long-term aim of one day rebuilding and reopening the branch, and thus reinstating the long-lost through connection from East Grinstead to Haywards Heath. A second-hand girder span has been acquired to replace the demolished Sheriff Mill Viaduct and a route round the edge of the depot at Ardingly has been safeguarded to allow the possibility of Bluebell trains passing the site of the former station. Even the possibility of re-electrifying the branch has not been ruled out, raising the unique prospect of seeing preserved electric trains one day operating under their own power on a UK heritage railway.

The route towards London

In addition to the Ardingly branch, the other element that was necessary to make the northern half of the Lewes & East Grinstead Railway a viable diversionary route for the Brighton line was, of course, a line north towards London. This was one of the nascent LEGR's original aims when the Earl of Sheffield held the first preliminary meeting of interested parties in

RIGHT The Bluebell Railway's very first items of rolling stock, 'Terrier' No 55 *Stepney* and coaches Nos S320 and S6575 pass through Copyhold Junction on 17 May 1960, en route for Sheffield Park and their new life in preservation. If the Bluebell's future plans come to fruition, it may only be a matter of time before steam trains once again appear on the Ardingly branch. *Derek Cross, Bluebell Railway Museum Archive*

September 1876, and in October of that year John Wolfe Barry, the line's Engineer, was instructed to proceed with surveying the entire route from Lewes through to Croydon. The proposed route was to incorporate parts of the abandoned works from the never completed Surrey & Sussex Junction Railway, and was to enter into the territory of the South Eastern Railway in the vicinity of Godstone. Unfortunately, this encroachment was to prove a major stumbling block for the LBSCR, which was happy to let the Lewes to East Grinstead proposal pass through Parliament unopposed but could not be seen to support any railway that penetrated into the territory of its great rival.

Initially the LEGR directors determined to press ahead with their route north of East Grinstead, regardless of the opinion of the LBSCR but, as the months went by and financial realities pressed home, they were forced to climb down. By the end of 1877 the LEGR had effectively been taken over by the LBSCR and the proposed northern extension had been abandoned.

Having seen off the LEGR's proposal, the LBSCR promptly set about making its own plans to extend the line north from East Grinstead, this time working in cooperation with the SER, and in 1878 an Act was passed by Parliament for a Croydon, Oxted & East Grinstead line. Using a route similar to that proposed by Wolfe Barry, and again utilising parts of the abandoned SSJR line, the new line was to be engineered by Frederick Bannister of the LBSCR and, like the LEGR, constructed by Joseph Firbank. Opening for traffic in March 1884, a year and a half after the first train from Lewes had arrived at East Grinstead, the new line was solely owned by the LBSCR as far north as Hurst Green, and beyond there jointly owned and operated with the SER. Finally it was possible for through trains from London to travel via East Grinstead to Lewes or, via the Ardingly line, to Brighton.

Often in railway history it was the later lines to be built that were among the first to close, being frequently the least necessary routes and so least likely to succeed financially. In this instance East Grinstead bucked the trend, for of the four routes radiating from the town it was the last built, the line to London, that served the greatest purpose and was to outlive all of its predecessors. Following the final closure of the erstwhile LEGR in 1958, the routes to the east and west fell victim to local resident Dr Richard Beeching, being named in his *Reshaping of British Railways* report published in 1963. The east-west route finally closed on 1 January 1967, leaving the Oxted line as East Grinstead's final surviving link to the national rail network.

Electrification and beyond

The extension of the third-rail electric network from Horsted Keynes to East Grinstead and northwards was first considered in 1939. In the event it was to be 1987 before the first electric service arrived into East Grinstead from the north, services having been provided by DEMUs since the 1960s. East Grinstead had finally joined the former Southern Electric network, but almost a quarter of a century too late to save the fortunes of the Ardingly branch.

Steam returned to East Grinstead, from the south, when the Bluebell Railway's northern extension opened throughout in 2013, the first timetabled passenger service arriving in March of that year. The connection of the Bluebell to the national network at East Grinstead means that once again through trains, in the form of steam- or diesel-hauled specials, are able to operate from London or elsewhere to Horsted Keynes and Sheffield Park. The prospect of the Bluebell reopening the Ardingly branch raises the possibility that passengers may one day again be able to board a train from London, via East Grinstead and Horsted Keynes, to Haywards Heath, or even onward to Brighton.

CHAPTER FOUR

. . . .

A railway in decline

The Lewes to East Grinstead line in the early decades of the 20th century was a railway that had never really achieved the potential its founders had hoped for. Unlike some areas, where the building of a railway had proved a spur for residential development, the villages served by the former LEGR remained small hamlets, meaning that passenger numbers remained low. Goods traffic, which originally formed a considerable part of the line's traffic, soon went into decline in the years following the First World War, as local farmers and producers switched to the convenience of mechanised road transport. The scope for using the northern section of the line as a relief route, via the Ardingly branch, was arguably never fully realised, and the electrification in 1935 of the branch only was a lost opportunity that reinforced the separation of the branch from the Lewes to East Grinstead line.

Newick & Chailey Station. L. B. & S. C. R.

ABOVE A colourised postcard view of LBSCR 'Terrier' No 81 *Beulah*, temporarily converted to a 2-4-0T, calling at Newick & Chailey with a Marsh 'balloon' coach – essentially a 'motor-train'-style service. The date of the photo is unknown but interestingly the card was posted in 1907, two years before railmotor services are generally supposed to have begun over the southern section of the line. *Bluebell Railway Museum Archive*

LBSCR economies

Probably the first economy measure introduced by the LBSCR was the entry into service of 'railmotor' services over the southern section of the line, from Horsted Keynes to Lewes, in 1909. Cheap to operate, these initially consisted of a single Marsh 'Balloon' coach hauled by one of the diminutive 'Terrier' Class of locomotives. Two of the class, Nos 681 *Beulah* and 682 *Boxhill* were temporarily modified to 2-4-0Ts to operate this service, while other regular performers included No 655 *Stepney* – later to achieve fame as the first ever loco to be preserved by the Bluebell Railway.

The first signs of infrastructure rationalisation occurred at Horsted Keynes in 1914, and by the end of the First World War the station had lost one of its two signal boxes and all buildings and canopies on the furthermost island platform. Hand-in-hand with these changes went the rearrangement of the junction's trackwork and signalling so that the potentially important route via Ardingly to Haywards Heath and Brighton was now relegated to branch status while the single-track route south to Lewes had now become the de facto main line. Further economies occurred at Barcombe in 1916 when the station master there also took over responsibility for nearby Barcombe Mills station on the Uckfield line – perhaps initially intended as a wartime economy, this twinning of stations would set the trend for further such arrangements in peacetime.

LEFT At the turn of the last century LBSCR 'B1' Class No 185 *George A. Wallis* pauses at Barcombe with a southbound Victoria-Brighton train. *Bluebell Railway Museum Archive*

ABOVE In 1922, the last year of the pre-Grouping era, LBSCR Class 'E4' No 475 passes East Grinstead North box as it shunts the stock of the 1.25pm Brighton to East Grinstead train to form the 3.07pm service to Haywards Heath. *Bluebell Railway Museum Archive*

BELOW Ex-LBSCR 'E4' Class No B491 enters Haywards Heath with a local service off the Ardingly branch on 19 July 1930. *H. C. Casserley, Bluebell Railway Museum Archive*

Grouping

The grouping of the line, together with the rest of the LBSCR, into the new Southern Railway in 1923 made little difference to the former LEGR; service levels and rolling stock remained largely unchanged and economy measures continued. The arrangement at Barcombe had proved that there was scope for employing fewer station masters on the line and 1926 saw both Ardingly and West Hoathly placed under the control of Horsted Keynes, while Kingscote found itself under the wing of East Grinstead.

In the 1930s, with the economy in recession, the pace of cutbacks increased. Changes at Barcombe in 1931 saw responsibility for

ABOVE **A 1935 shot of ex-LBSCR 'B4' Class 4-4-0 No 2042 heading south from Horsted Keynes.** *Ian C. Allen, Bluebell Railway Museum Archive*

BELOW **Electrification of the Ardingly branch could have led to further extension of the third rail from Horsted Keynes to East Grinstead and beyond. Sadly, by the time this photo of 2-NOL unit No 1818 leaving Horsted Keynes was taken in 1957 any such plans had long been postponed indefinitely and the future of the branch was already looking bleak.** *Neil Sprinks, Bluebell Railway Museum Archive*

Barcombe Mills taken over by another Uckfield line station, while Barcombe itself, together with Newick & Chailey, was now placed under the control of the station master at Sheffield Park. More visible economies occurred the following year when Barcombe lost its sole signal box and part of its canopies, while in 1934 Sheffield Park in turn lost both of its signal boxes in favour of a ground frame on the platform. The significance of Sheffield Park had, of course, been greatly diminished since the death of the Earl of Sheffield in the Edwardian era and further demolition was to follow there in the late 1940s when the station was deprived of its footbridge. In the meantime Newick & Chailey lost both of its signal boxes in 1938, together with all of the buildings on the up platform, the up line at this station now being relegated to a loop siding.

Electrification

The one part of the former LEGR system to receive significant investment in the 1930s was of course the Ardingly branch. This arrived in the form of the electrification scheme of 1935, but even this was to prove something of a two-edged sword. If anything the electrification from Haywards Heath to Horsted

ABOVE Ex-LBSCR 'D1' Class No 2221 prepares to leave Horsted Keynes with a railmotor service for Haywards Heath on 18 August 1934. Electrification of the Ardingly branch the following year would mean that in future all services for the branch would depart from the exposed position of the furthermost island platform. *H. J. Wheeler, Bluebell Railway Museum Archive*

BELOW An unidentified 'U1' Class locomotive emerges from the southern end of Cinder Hill Tunnel on 26 March 1955. It was in this same tunnel that another train, headed by 'D3' Class No 2372, sought refuge when targeted by a German plane on 16 December 1942. *Pamlin Prints, Bluebell Railway Museum Archive*

Keynes was a missed opportunity, serving only to emphasise the branch as a separate entity from the 'main' Lewes to East Grinstead route. From now on it would have been impossible for timetablers to extend the local services from Haywards Heath beyond Horsted Keynes, even if they had felt reason to do so. Likewise the potential to use the route north of Horsted Keynes as a diversionary route for the Brighton line, itself electrified since 1933, was greatly reduced.

Clearly this potential was recognised by the upper levels of the Southern Railway in 1939 when plans were formed to extend the electrification from Horsted Keynes, through East Grinstead, to join with the existing third-rail network at Sanderstead. Unfortunately dark clouds were descending across Europe by this time and the proposal was indefinitely postponed by the outbreak of the Second World War.

Second World War

The outbreak of war did not bring huge changes to the Lewes to East Grinstead route. Although the South East of England was effectively on the front line of hostilities, the still predominantly rural nature of the area between Lewes and East Grinstead meant that the line was largely immune from the heavy bombing that targeted the towns and cities. Some bomb damage was occasionally sustained to the trackbed, although none of the stations sustained a direct hit, and bomb damage elsewhere did from time to time see the line used as a diversion for other nearby routes. Also sent via the Ardingly

branch were munitions trains from Newhaven, a practice that had previously occurred during the First World War.

The relative safety from bombing that the line was able to offer meant that unused siding space was utilised for the storage of military items that may have been at risk of loss or damage if held in more conventional locations. A trainload of tanks was for a time berthed at Kingscote, while the sidings at Horsted Keynes played host at various times to such items as ships' propellers, tank parts and ammunition trains. Also held at Horsted Keynes, for much the same reasons, were items of rolling stock, frequently Pullman cars, made temporarily redundant by the war, and which the authorities deemed to be too vulnerable if kept in Brighton's Preston Park depot.

One particularly dramatic event that did occur on the line during the war took place on 16 December 1942 when a northbound passenger train was pursued and machine-gunned by a German aircraft midway between Barcombe and Newick & Chailey. One of the passengers suffered serious facial wounds in the attack, but thanks to the efforts of the footplate crew the train, which was headed by 'D3' Class No 2372, was able to take refuge in Cinder Hill Tunnel before any greater tragedies could occur.

Another wartime event was a Civil Defence exercise held immediately to the south of West Hoathly Tunnel on 18 April 1943, apparently a practice run for carrying out permanent way repairs in the aftermath of a simulated gas attack. Thankfully such an attack never became a reality but the exercise, which was recorded for posterity by an official photographer, is notable because, despite the usual cloak of secrecy that surrounded military matters in wartime, the whole operation was carried out within full view of a crowd of local spectators!

Peacetime and nationalisation

Having been relatively untouched by the events of the Second World War, the Lewes to East Grinstead route that emerged into peacetime was one little changed since the 1920s. The electrified Ardingly branch finally overcame opposition to a Sunday Service in 1945, but the timetable between Lewes and East Grinstead had seen few revisions since the days of the LBSCR. In fact, so unchanged was the timetable of the late 1940s that trains were still being held for long periods at both Lewes and East Grinstead to allow for the loading of milk churns. In reality the milk traffic had long since been lost to the roads, meaning that staff were being forced to hold

BELOW One of a series of official photographs taken of the Civil Defence decontamination test exercise carried out to the south of Sharpthorne Tunnel on 18 April 1943. Two trains were involved, both hauled by unidentified Class 'C2X' 0-6-0s. *Bluebell Railway Museum Archive*

ABOVE While some sources differ as to the precise date of the demolition of Sheffield Park's original footbridge, it remains the case that this image from June 1949 may well be the last known view of the bridge still in situ. The poster on the right is advertising racing at Fontwell Park on Whit Monday, 6 June 1949. *Bluebell Railway Museum Archive*

passenger trains for the loading of non-existent goods that they knew full well hadn't materialised for years and were never going to come again.

One positive change that had occurred during the war, and which would have an impact on the various special trains that traversed the line in its final years, was the gradual lifting of weight restrictions. Prior to the 1940s the size of locomotives allowed over the lightly used line was quite restricted and it was largely the preserve of ex-LBSCR tank engines and other

smaller pre-Grouping locos. From 1943 onwards this was changed to allow Maunsell 2-6-0s and LBSCR 'K' Class engines to traverse the line, with further relaxations following to allow Bulleid's 'Light Pacifics' to use the route. The latter would go on to make a number of appearances on railtours and ramblers' specials over former LEGR metals in the 1950s.

Electrification of the line from Horsted Keynes to East Grinstead was given serious consideration again in 1947, but by this time the Southern Railway was in its final months of existence. On 1 January 1948 the company was nationalised as part of the newly created British Railways and a change of priorities, coupled with the harsh realities of post-war austerity, meant that electrification, first proposed in the 1930s, was once again kicked into the long grass. The railways were changing and time was rapidly running out for loss-making rural lines like the former Lewes & East Grinstead Railway.

CHAPTER FIVE

....

The beginning of the end

Nationalisation would initially mean little visible change for passengers on the Lewes to East Grinstead route. The pre-Grouping LBSCR and SECR locomotives that handled most of the trains were soon largely replaced by LMS-designed Class 2 and Class 4 tank engines (BR Standard Class 4 tanks would also later appear), but otherwise things remained much as before. Behind the scenes, however, the mood was changing. Within seven years of the creation of British Railways, the line closed for the first time.

Economic review

In the harsh economic reality of post-war Britain the newly created British Transport Commission (BTC) quickly found itself faced with spiralling losses and, with some justification, it was underused local branch lines that took the brunt of the blame. From the early 1950s BTC officials were actively reviewing the costs and income of freight and passenger traffic on rural railways across much of the UK, and the branches of Sussex were no exception. Savings were required and something had to go.

When passenger services were withdrawn on the Kent & East Sussex Railway in 1953 the *Sussex Express & County Herald* reported that 'the fate of other branch lines in Sussex which are under "economic review" is still hanging in the balance.' Among several other lines listed by the paper as being under potential threat was the Lewes to East Grinstead route. Having enquired at the Public Relations Department at Waterloo as to the fate of these lines, a reporter had been advised that it was 'impossible to say when a decision will be reached on the fate of these lines which have already been under consideration for two years… If the economic review is felt to justify curtailment, they may be partly or entirely closed.'

ABOVE Ex-LBSCR 'E4' Class 0-6-2T No 32520, sister to the Bluebell Railway's own *Birch Grove*, pulls out of Barcombe during 1953, the year in which concerns began to be raised concerning the future of the Lewes to East Grinstead line. Two years later Barcombe would close for good. *R. C. Riley, Bluebell Railway Museum Archive*

LEFT Still carrying Southern Railway livery and number, 'I1X' Class 4-4-2T No 2002, rebuilt in 1931 from an LBSCR Class 'I1', leaves Barcombe with the 4.03pm Lewes to Horsted Keynes service on 14 May 1951. The writing may have been on the wall for the Lewes to East Grinstead line, but it would at least outlive No 2002, which would be withdrawn only two months later in July 1951, the last survivor of its type. *J. J. Smith, Bluebell Railway Museum Archive*

BELOW Ramblers' excursion trains had been a feature of the Lewes to East Grinstead line since the 1930s, and the relaxation of weight restrictions that occurred during wartime allowed for a number of these to be hauled by Bulleid 'Pacifics' in the post-war years. On 22 March 1953 'Battle of Britain' Class No 34071 *601 Squadron* passes through East Grinstead with the 9.50am Victoria to Sheffield Park Ramblers' Special. *Bluebell Railway Museum Archive*

Remarking that the former Southern Railway's electrification programme had been indefinitely shelved, the paper gloomily concluded that 'It would appear that there are few hopes of any major improvements in East Sussex railways … for some time to come.'[10]

Closure recommendation

For the Lewes to East Grinstead line the bombshell dropped in May 1954 when the Southern Region of British Railways announced its intention to close the line with the publication of a memorandum entitled 'Withdrawal of Services from East Grinstead and Lewes'. The *Express & County Herald* covered the story in its 7 May edition, saying, 'After three years of

investigation and consideration British Railways have decided that the line is not a paying proposition and are recommending its closure.' Such a decision needed to be referred to the Transport Users' Consultative Committee (South Eastern area) for its approval before services could actually be withdrawn, and a BTC spokesman was quoted as saying that 'Local councils, traders, chambers of commerce have been fully aware of our investigations and they, too, will be able to put forward their arguments and suggestions to the committee.' Regarding another local line that was perceived to be under threat, the East Grinstead to Tunbridge Wells line (which in fact was to survive until the 1960s before closure), the spokesman remarked, 'That line is still under consideration but we have reached a decision on the East Grinstead to Barcombe line. Our decision to recommend its closure will be placed before the next meeting of the Consultative Committee.'[11]

A statement issued by the BTC on 10 June 1954 announced that, subject to approval from the licensing authority, the local bus company, Southdown Motor Services, would be introducing additional buses on existing routes to make up for the loss of the train service. Attempting to appease growing local opposition, the BTC, paraphrased by the local paper, was keen to advise that, other than Sheffield Park, 'all the places served by the branch line have buses connecting them with either Lewes, Haywards Heath or East Grinstead.' (As we shall see, this argument would soon be given short shrift by local people.) Barcombe, it was pointed out, was also served by trains calling at Barcombe Mills station (on the Uckfield line), while Haywards Heath would continue to be served by trains on the electrified Ardingly branch. Although there was no direct bus route linking Lewes and East Grinstead, journeys between the two towns would still be possible 'by train, or train and bus, via Haywards Heath and Three Bridges.'[12]

Local opposition

The alternatives suggested by the British Transport Commission fell far short of adequate as far as the local authorities and people were concerned. For the rest of the year reports of individual complaints, protest meetings and hostile local councils continued to occupy column inches in the pages of the *Sussex Express & County Herald*. A protest meeting organised by the East Grinstead Urban Council in June was attended by representatives from local authorities, political

BELOW 'D3' Class 0-4-4T No 32390 prepares to run round its train before departing from Lewes with an RCTS railtour for Tunbridge Wells, via Sheffield Park, on 4 October 1953. Another former LBSCR loco destined to be the last of its type, No 32390 was cut up two years later, in October 1955. *Bluebell Railway Museum Archive*

LEFT The rapid decline in goods traffic over the first half of the 20th century had certainly helped to sound the death knell for the Lewes to East Grinstead line. Ex-LBSCR 'C2X' Class No 32540 is not troubled by a heavy load as it departs from Horsted Keynes with the 11.20am West Hoathly to Lewes freight service on 23 October 1953. *Neil Sprinks, Bluebell Railway Museum Archive*

ABOVE Ivatt 2-6-2T No 41307 takes water at Sheffield Park at the head of the southbound 3.35pm Oxted to Brighton service in June 1954. In the up platform is 'birdcage' set No 616 headed by 'C2X' Class No 32536 with the 4.03pm Lewes to Horsted Keynes service. *Peter Hay, Bluebell Railway Museum Archive*

parties, social clubs and trade organisations along the route. Groups as diverse as the Women's Institute and the Communist Party lined up in their joint opposition to the proposed closure; a local Liberal Party spokeswoman described the BTC's plans as 'criminal lunacy'. Also present at the meeting were representatives of the BTC itself, who revealed that according to their figures closure of the line would result in a net saving of £59,000 per annum – total receipts being estimated at only £9,000 against a current annual expenditure of £68,000. Speaking on behalf of the BTC, Mr J. Bridger, Chief District Superintendent at Redhill, bemoaned the fact that these losses were in effect the fault of a local population who had long since deserted the line in favour of local motor bus services: 'These buses have been a convenience to you and you have left the railway, and that is why we find ourselves in this position today.'[13]

A common thread running through much of the local opposition to the closure of the line was that the replacement bus services proposed would be hopelessly inadequate – while local roads would be unable to cope with the volume of traffic generated by the loss of railway goods facilities. A report from 6 August reveals that, while Chailey Parish Council was apparently unconcerned by the proposed closure, the members of Barcombe Parish Council were firmly of the position that, in the words of the local rector, 'We want more trains not more buses.' Newick Parish Council was more amenable to the idea of more buses, but asked for significant improvements in local bus services, above and beyond what the BTC was currently offering, as well as the erection of more bus shelters.[14] A similar desire for more shelters and improved bus services had already been expressed by Fletching Parish Council, a resolution passed in June announcing that if these improvements were carried out 'the suspension of passenger traffic on the railway line through Sheffield Park would be reasonable' – but provided also that the goods service on the line was retained in full![15] In July two local residents wrote to the BTC's Chief Administrative Officer bemoaning the inadequacy of the planned bus service and demanding to know 'what guarantee can the British Railways give to the public that the proposed extra bus service, or even the present bus service, will continue to run?'[16] The letter, which was quoted at length in the *Express & County Herald*, is notable for its suggestion that the nationalised railway should provide a public service, like the Post Office, regardless of profit or loss, and also for the fact that one of its joint signatories was a Miss R. E. M. Bessemer of North Chailey. Miss Bessemer would soon prove to be a very painful thorn in the side of the BTC.

'Even if [the replacement bus services] were sufficient there would be much inconvenience to travellers,' stated Mr B. Dutton Briant QC to Newick Parish Council in early November 1954. Mr Briant's comments were significant because at that stage he was expected to soon be representing the Parish Council at the inquiry into the proposed closure (in the event his appointment as a County Court Judge would see him

replaced in this role). Taking issue with the 'completely unreliable' figures provided by the BTC, he queried how a reported 183,000 passengers per year could result in only £8,000 takings, or less than 1 shilling per journey, 'and that did not take into consideration revenue from goods.' Describing the closure of the line as anything but a foregone conclusion, he stated with remarkably accurate foresight that British Railways 'might find the position different from other places. I am not at all satisfied that the closing is going to come off as quickly as the railways think.' Meanwhile East Sussex County Council was taking the rather more pragmatic approach of inquiring what would happen to the land once the line had closed.[17]

The TUCC inquiry

The fate of the Lewes to East Grinstead line was sealed, or so it seemed, when the Transport Users' Consultative Committee held its inquiry into the proposed closure at the Charing Cross Hotel on 30 November 1954. The meeting was reported at length in the *Sussex Express & County Herald*[18], but the arguments put to the TUCC, both for and against, would have already been familiar to its readers, having already been well-rehearsed by the BTC and local protesters over the preceding seven months.

Replacing the recently promoted Mr Dutton Briant, the protest deputation was led by Mr David Peck, a barrister from Newick. Equally scathing and belligerent as his predecessor in

BELOW Brand-new BR Standard Class 4MT 2-6-4T No 80105 is about to enter Sharpthorne Tunnel as it departs south from West Hoathly on 30 April 1955 with coach set No 956 forming the 12.03pm Victoria to Brighton service. A product of Brighton Works, No 80105 is seen here being run in before initially being allocated to the London, Tilbury & Southend line. Withdrawn after a career of only 10 years, the loco was ultimately rescued from Barry scrapyard in 1975 and currently resides in Scotland at the Bo'ness & Kinneil Railway.
R. C. Riley, Bluebell Railway Museum Archive

ABOVE Less than a week before closure, Fairburn Class 4 2-6-4T No 42104 heads south near Kingscote with the 4.20pm London Bridge to Brighton service on 23 May 1955. *J. Head, Bluebell Railway Museum Archive*

his criticism of the BTC, Mr Peck, in the words of the newspaper, refused even to concede 'that … the Transport Commission had power to close the Lewes-East Grinstead route'. In summary, his main arguments were as follows:

- That the BTC should continue to operate loss-making routes as a public service, subsidising them with the surplus income from other, profitable, routes.
- That the figures produced by the BTC were unreliable and failed to account adequately for goods traffic, or for passenger journeys starting at locations outside the Lewes to East Grinstead route.
- That the BTC's own figure of 180,000 passenger journeys per year, although not to be accepted at face value, was in itself justification for retaining the railway line.
- That the upsurge in local journeys by car and bus was largely due to the inadequacy of the service currently operated on the railway. Pre-war service levels, argued Mr Peck, had not been restored after the cessation of hostilities.
- That the importance of the route via Haywards Heath as a diversionary route for the main London-Brighton line had been proved during the Second World War and could be a valuable alternative during peacetime also.
- That the Southern Railway's pre-war electrification plans proved that the line, if not actually profitable at

the time, was at least seen then as having a viable long-term future.
- That the proposed improvement to local bus services was not an adequate replacement for the railway service, would be inconvenient for mothers travelling with children and prams, and made no provision for the loss of goods facilities.

Other opponents to the closure who spoke at the meeting included Mr B. W. Howe of Home Farm, Sheffield Park, who stated that journey times on the line were unchanged since he was a boy, and queried whether savings couldn't be made by reintroducing push-pull services and converting the Horsted Keynes to East Grinstead section to single track? Also present was the Rev W. P. Webb of Barcombe, who stated that the local roads were inadequate for an increased bus service and expressed his own support for electrifying the line before presenting a petition signed by 1,400 individuals opposed to the closure.

If the protestors' arguments were already familiar, the BTC was equally intransigent. Seemingly presenting its case to the committee by way of a memorandum, the BTC was sticking to its original figures – the line was claimed to make only £9,000 per year, meaning that an estimated annual saving of £59,000 could be effected by its closure. Additional buses were to be provided by Southdown Motor Services on existing routes only, while for goods traffic, 'Collection and delivery services for freight and parcels will be continued throughout the area. Railheads for bulk traffics will remain available at Barcombe Mills, Uckfield, Cooksbridge, Horsted Keynes and East Grinstead.' In other words, several months of protest had apparently achieved nothing and what was on the table now was exactly the same as had been announced back in May.

The TUCC decision

Faced with the black-and-white reality of the BTC's official figures, however disputed in some quarters, the decision of the Transport Users' Consultative Committee (South Eastern) was perhaps more of a foregone conclusion than some would have hoped. After meeting with protestors for 3½ hours, and a

further hour deliberating in private, the committee came to its decision: the TUCC was to support the BTC's decision and to make a recommendation to the Minister of Transport that the Lewes to East Grinstead line be approved for closure.

The end?

The end, or so it seemed at the time, of the Lewes to East Grinstead line came not so much with a bang as with a whimper. With the BTC's decision approved by the TUCC, the Minister of Transport's agreement was a formality and a closure date was soon set for 13 June 1955. An RCTS railtour was arranged to traverse the line on the final day, but events were soon to intervene that meant the line would close early and without ceremony.

A national enginemen's strike called by ASLEF meant that the last regular passenger trains ran over the line on Sunday 28 May 1955, two weeks before the official closure date. No commemorations were held and few were there to witness the departure of the final southbound train from East Grinstead at 8.38pm and the final northbound train from Lewes at 10.06pm. It seemed that the old Lewes & East Grinstead Railway, save for its branch from Horsted Keynes to Haywards Heath, had passed into history unnoticed and unremarked.

With the ASLEF strike not affecting station staff, the stations between Lewes and East Grinstead remained staffed until the 'official' closure date of 13 June – ticket offices open

BELOW With the official closure of the line not due to take place for another two weeks, the actual last day of operation, brought forward by the onset of an ASLEF strike, passed with little ceremony on 28 May 1955. Photographed on the final day, ex-LBSCR 'E4' Class No 32508 approaches Newick & Chailey with the 7.28pm train to Lewes. *M. J. Esau, Bluebell Railway Museum Archive*

ABOVE Originally scheduled to run on the official 'last day' but delayed by the ASLEF strike, Brighton 'H2' Class 'Atlantic' No 32426 *St Alban's Head* passes near Newick & Chailey with 'The Wealden Limited' RCTS railtour on 14 August 1955. Few on that date could have imagined that regular passenger services over the line would resume less than 12 months later. *J. H. W. Kent, Bluebell Railway Museum Archive*

to sell tickets to passengers that would never come for journeys that could never be undertaken. (Reportedly a brisk trade was done in the sale of tickets, largely by mail order, to enthusiasts keen to purchase a final souvenir before the line officially passed away.) The RCTS railtour, booked for the final day, was still under contract to run and once the strike was over was finally allowed to proceed on 14 August. Crowds turned out to witness the passage of 'The Wealden Limited', hauled by LBSCR 'H2' Class 'Atlantic' No 32426 *St Alban's Head* immaculately turned out by Brighton shed, as it traversed the line between Lewes and East Grinstead a full two months after the official closure date had passed.

And that was that, the end of the Lewes to East Grinstead railway line – or at least it would have been but for a remarkable turn of events that would see the British Transport Commission forced to recommence passenger services over the line a mere 12 months after the farewell railtour had passed…

CHAPTER SIX

· · · · · · · · · · · · · · · · ·

A temporary reprieve

In August 1956 a photograph of a two-coach train headed by 'C2X' Class

No 32442 appeared in *The Illustrated London News* above the following caption:

'BETWEEN SHEFFIELD PARK AND HORSTED KEYNES: THE FIRST

TRAIN PASSING ALONG THE REOPENED "BLUEBELL AND PRIMROSE"

BRANCH LINE IN SUSSEX. On August 7 British Railways reopened the "Bluebell

and Primrose" branch line between East Grinstead and Lewes. Local inhabitants,

who had protested against the closure of the line, crowded every station along

the seventeen miles to wave and cheer the first train.'[19]

ABOVE 7 August 1956 – re-opening day! The first up train of the revived service, hauled by ex-LBSCR 'K' Class 2-6-0 No 32342, calls at Newick & Chailey, Madge Bessemer's local station. The disused former up platform can be seen on the right while the lady on the left appears to be taking down the loco number – perhaps for the benefit of her young son? *Hugh Davies, Bluebell Railway Museum Archive*

LEFT The British Railways poster announcing that the Lewes-East Grinstead line was to re-open on 7 August 1956. *Neil Sprinks, Bluebell Railway Museum Archive*

This brief report raises three questions. Why had the British Transport Commission reopened a line it had been so keen to close only one year before? Why were events on a sleepy branch line in rural Sussex now attracting the attention of the London press? And why was the former Lewes & East Grinstead Railway now being referred to in the media as the 'Bluebell and Primrose' line?

Why did the British Transport Commission reopen the line?

In May 1955 Bill Howe of Home Farm, Sheffield Park, wrote to the BTC enquiring whether the railway cottages at the local station would be available for purchase following closure of the line. The reply he received included the statement that 'the track shall remain in situ for a period of 12 months from the date of closure in case some subsequent development necessitates reconsideration of the abandonment of the line.'[20] This precaution would, as it turned out, prove vital in view of the embarrassing volte face that the BTC was about to make. For the future of the Lewes to East Grinstead line was about to be secured, at least temporarily, by the efforts of one woman, Miss R. E. M. 'Madge' Bessemer.

Madge Bessemer

Aged around 60, Miss Bessemer was the granddaughter of the Victorian industrialist Sir Henry Bessemer (whose invention of the Bessemer process had revolutionised the mass-production of steel in the latter half of the 19th century) and a prominent resident of North Chailey. A member of the Parish Council, when the line that ran past her estate came under threat of closure in 1954 she was quick to respond, forming a 'Fighting Committee' that also included the Rev W. P. Webb of Barcombe (who was later to address the TUCC inquiry in November of that year) among its members. Her correspondence on the matter with the British Transport Commission was to form the basis of at least two articles in the *Sussex Express & County Herald* in July 1954. A car-owner herself, whether Miss Bessemer was a regular user of the railway is unclear but, whatever her motivations, one thing that is certain is that she was determined to be a thorn in the side of the BTC. (In 1959, some years after the events recounted in this chapter, she was quoted in the national press over her opposition to the BTC's proposed suspension of the Newhaven to Dieppe ferry service – despite the fact that, by her own admission, she had not used that service since before the Second World War!)[21]

ABOVE A busy scene at East Grinstead station on the first day of the revived Lewes to East Grinstead service. Ex-LBSCR 'C2X' Class 0-6-0 No 32442 has run round its two-car train from Lewes before manoeuvring into the down platform for the return journey. Above it, 'M7' No 30052 can be seen in the High Level platforms at the head of a train to Three Bridges. *T. Wright, Bluebell Railway Museum Archive*

An illegal closure

Unsatisfied with the outcome of the TUCC inquiry in November 1954, Miss Bessemer continued to campaign against the closure throughout 1955. Having obtained copies of the Parliamentary Acts authorising the construction of the Lewes & East Grinstead Railway from the Public Record Office, she, with the aid of her lawyers, made a momentous discovery. Under Section 35 of the 1878 London, Brighton & South Coast Railway (Croydon, Oxted & East Grinstead Railways) Act it appeared that the LBSCR, and by implication its successors, was legally obliged to provide a passenger service of four trains a day over the line. In other words, since the 1878 Act had never been repealed, the closure of 1955 was, technically, illegal. Armed with this knowledge, Miss Bessemer and her solicitors wasted no time in communicating the fact to the BTC, the Ministry of Transport, and the press.

On 28 April 1956 *The Guardian* announced:

'Reports from Lewes to-day suggest that British Railways may have to re-open six stations and seventeen miles of track connecting East Grinstead with Kingscote, West Hoathly, Sheffield Park, Newick and Chailey, Barcombe Junction, and Lewes... This morning the principal objectors to the closing of the line, led by Miss Bessemer, of North Chailey, near Lewes, took heart from reports that their plans had been successful. They had based their case on the theory that the line could be closed only by act of parliament. This evening the Ministry of Transport could only say that the Minister, Mr Harold Watkinson, had had a letter from Miss Bessemer's solicitor and was considering it... Whatever the results of Ministerial attention, the supporters of the line seemed confident of victory.'[22]

The supporters of the line were right to sense that victory was within their grasp, and a follow-up article on 13 June confirmed that the BTC had conceded that Miss Bessemer's point was valid; closing the line without the approval of Parliament was, it seemed, technically illegal. Taking a more cautionary tone, however, the paper recorded that the Minister of Transport had pointed out that the original Act could be amended and the line then closed legally. Since this would take time, asks the article, 'would the commission have to reopen it and wait for Parliament's permission to close it properly?'[23] The answer would ultimately prove to be 'yes'. In the meantime, on 1 June 1956, a weedkilling train had appeared on the line hauled by 'K' Class No 32350, apparently clearing the permanent way for a resumption of services.

Why was the media interested?

The original closure of the Lewes to East Grinstead line in 1955 had apparently attracted little attention outside of the pages of the local newspapers, but the following year, with the line's reopening seemingly imminent, the national media started to take an increasing interest. Many rural railway lines were closing around this time, so why did this one line start to attract so much attention? Needless to say, the British press love an underdog, especially one that can seemingly take on the supposedly faceless bureaucrats of Whitehall and win – and the supporters of the Lewes to East Grinstead line looked

to be doing just that. Not only that, but the old LEGR had a catchy nickname – 'The Bluebell Line' (see below for why this was) – which was rapidly gaining traction in the national consciousness. This was, after all, the era of *The Titfield Thunderbolt*, the 1953 film (itself inspired by real events on the Talyllyn Railway in mid-Wales), in which a group of plucky locals successfully prevent the Ministry of Transport from closing their local branch line. In the events unfolding on the Lewes to East Grinstead line, the press had discovered their own real-life Titfield – plucky locals, an idiosyncratic nickname and a railway that was seemingly able to overcome the machinations of penny-pinching authority figures who wanted to close it down. Around 3,000 miles of railway were closed by the British Transport Commission over the course of the 1950s, but it was the Bluebell Line that had become the 'poster-girl' of the threatened rural branch.

Why 'The Bluebell Line'?

'It was largely through him guaranteeing a good deal of the money that our "bluebell railway line" was laid down,' said Mr Ballard. 'But now, unfortunately, we have no Lord Sheffield, and soon I am afraid the "bluebell line" will have to go as well.'[24]

Taken from an article in the 5 November 1954 edition of the *Sussex Express & County Herald*, the above quote is a relatively

early published use of a nickname that was soon to become forever synonymous with the Lewes to East Grinstead line. The name 'Bluebell Line' or 'Bluebell and Primrose Line', to give the full version, was obviously derived from the flowers that grew alongside the line and was presumably long-used by the locals (certainly the above-quoted Mr Ballard is using it in the sense of a long-familiar name). Klaus Marx recounts how it dated back to the days of the LBSCR and may in part have derived from stories that the trains stopped for so long en route that the passengers had time to get off and pick the flowers.[25] (This 'trains so slow you had time to get off and pick flowers' story may well have attached itself to many rural branch lines. Certainly this author's grandfather lived on the Isle of Wight and used to recount exactly the same the story regarding the former steam trains there.)

Whatever the origins of the name, it is clear that it was not in regular use in 1954. The threatened closure of the Lewes to East Grinstead line generated many articles in the *Sussex Express & County Herald* throughout 1954, yet the above example, taken from an article about a local cricket club, appears to be the only appearance of the phrase 'bluebell line' in the paper that year. (Similarly, in the same year it was possible for *The Railway Magazine* to publish a nine-page article about the line without once mentioning bluebells or primroses.[26]) However, from 1956, with the line increasingly gaining national fame, the 'Bluebell' name also rose to prominence. The media clearly found the name 'Lewes and East Grinstead line' too much of a mouthful and the old local nickname gave them an attractive and easily memorable

alternative. Soon it was impossible for newspapers, local or national, to mention the line without referring to it as the 'Bluebell and Primrose' line or, even more catchy, just plain 'Bluebell' line. By the end of the decade, even readers on the other side of the Atlantic were being regaled with articles about the famous 'Bluebell line'. In 1959 the adoption of the name by the preservation movement meant that the name Bluebell would be forever associated with the old Lewes to East Grinstead route.

Reopening

On 7 August 1956, just over 14 months since the last regular service had run, the now-famous Bluebell line reopened in a blaze of publicity. The first train, hauled by 'K' Class No 32342, departed from Lewes at 9.30am, its two coaches packed with locals, enthusiasts and the press. Madge Bessemer was now a local, if not national, celebrity, and was greeted by newspaper reporters and the BBC as she boarded the train at her local station of Newick & Chailey. Yet for all the celebrations, the protestors' triumph over the BTC was to prove a hollow victory.

RIGHT Viewed from the High Level platforms, 'C2X' Class No 32442 is seen again preparing to depart from East Grinstead on 2 September 1956 with the 4.28pm service to Lewes. Note the ex-LBSCR two-car 'push-pull' set, here being used as conventional hauled stock. Such was the unpopularity of the 'sulky service' that even two-coach formations were soon realised to be over-ambitious. *Neil Sprinks, Bluebell Railway Museum Archive*

If the protestors had hoped that a chastened BTC would attempt to improve services on the reopened line to win back traffic from the bus and motor car they were to be cruelly disappointed. Likewise any hope that the BTC could be persuaded to operate a loss-making service for the public benefit, funded at the expense of profitable services elsewhere, was unfounded. (In fairness to the Commission, this latter choice was never really an option as profitable services were somewhat thin on the ground for the BTC in the 1950s.) Instead, as predicted by *The Guardian* back in June, the BTC was merely biding its time, temporarily reopening the line against its better judgement until such time as it could close it again legally. The threat of closure continued to hang over the line as much now in 1956 as it had in 1954.

'Sulky service'

One lesson that the British Transport Commission had learned since 1954 was the importance of familiarising itself with the original enabling Acts of the LEGR and following the letter of the law. In particular the BTC had noted that it was only obliged to provide four passenger trains a day in each direction (and these to run entirely at a time of its own choosing). Moreover, these four trains a day were only obliged to call at Newick & Chailey, Sheffield Park, Horsted Keynes and West Hoathly.

Thus it was that the service that recommenced in August 1956, which quickly earned itself the derisory nickname of 'the sulky service', might have been almost deliberately designed to deter passengers from using the line (which in truth it probably was). A mere four trains a day departed from Lewes for East Grinstead, all of them between the hours of 9.30am and 3.30pm. Likewise the earliest return journey from East Grinstead to Lewes departed at 10.28am, the final departure being only 6 hours later at 4.28pm. Needless to say, these times were hardly practical for anyone considering using the railway for the purpose of commuting to work or school. The former stations at Kingscote and Barcombe, not having been mentioned in the relevant Act, were omitted altogether, despite the latter having been previously one of the busiest on the line. For Kingscote it would be another four decades before a passenger train would call there again; Barcombe has not seen another train since the tracks were taken up in 1962.

Amidst the celebratory atmosphere, 383 passengers were recorded as having travelled over the line on the reopening day

ABOVE By 1957 train lengths on the Lewes to East Grinstead service had been reduced to a single coach. BR Standard Class 4MT No 80031 is in charge of the single-car 1.30pm Lewes to East Grinstead service as it emerges into West Hoathly from the northern portal of Sharpthorne Tunnel on 21 March 1957. Note the date '1881' still proudly displayed above the tunnel mouth. *Colin Hogg, Bluebell Railway Museum Archive*

of 7 August 1956. Within a few days the reality of the unattractive timetable had sunk in and passenger numbers had dropped to a tiny fraction of those carried on the first day, most trains recording only single-figure totals. The two-car sets provided proved woefully over-optimistic and single-carriage trains quickly became the norm. Its case proven, the BTC continued to make plans for a more permanent closure of the line. Yet for the Bluebell line the temporary reprieve gained by Madge Bessemer and her allies would ultimately buy enough time to lay the foundations for another unexpected resurrection.

CHAPTER SEVEN

···························

From British Railways
to Bluebell Railway

Having been reopened in August 1956 purely because of a legal technicality,
it was clear that the Lewes to East Grinstead line, now almost universally known as
the 'Bluebell line', was living on borrowed time. In the event it took a mere 17 months
for the British Transport Commission to resolve the legal issues and close the line
again. Yet this 17-month stay of execution, coupled with the line's new-found fame,
was to prove just long enough for a viable preservation movement to arise. By the end
of the decade the Bluebell line – or at least part of it – was due to reopen again.

TOP LEFT One of a number of railtours that traversed the East Grinstead to Lewes line in the 1950s was the LCGB's 'Southern Counties Limited' on 24 February 1957, which was temporarily halted at Horsted Keynes when Brighton 'Atlantic' No 32424 *Beachy Head* had to be removed from the train owing to big-end trouble. In the event the defective loco was replaced by 'C2X' Class No 32437. *Hugh Davies, Bluebell Railway Museum Archive*

TOP RIGHT The 12.28pm East Grinstead to Lewis service, hauled by ex-LBSCR 'C2X' Class No 32440, passes south through Imberhorne cutting on 21 March 1957. In the same month the BTC presented a Bill to Parliament that would allow it to repeal the statutory service levels required by the 1878 Act and so close the line altogether. *Colin Hogg, Bluebell Railway Museum Archive*

ABOVE RIGHT BR Standard 4MT No 80154, built at Brighton Works, is in its first year of operation as it heads north from Horsted Keynes with a single-car train in 1957. For the Lewes to East Grinstead route the end was already nigh. *Neil Sprinks, Bluebell Railway Museum Archive*

LEFT This rare colour shot from 1957 shows BR Standard tank Class 4MT No 80011 at Newick & Chailey with a down 'sulky service' train. *Neil Sprinks, Bluebell Railway Museum Archive*

Closure threat renewed

In March 1957 a Bill was presented to Parliament by the BTC that included a clause to repeal the statutory four-trains-a-day requirement imposed by the original 1878 Act. The stage was now set for the commission to close the line legally, and the rest of 1957 was to see a virtual repeat of 1954 as both BTC and protestors locked horns over the same arguments again. The intention to withdraw the service was formally announced in August 1957, subject to the result of a three-day enquiry to be held by the Central Transport Consultative Committee (CTCC) in October of that year.

The enquiry results, made public in a White Paper published in February 1958, made grim reading for supporters of the Lewes to East Grinstead line. 'The Central Transport Consultative Committee has recommended that the decision to close the "Bluebell Line" between East Grinstead and Lewes should be

upheld,' stated *The Guardian* on 13 February.[27] Revealing that, excluding the towns of East Grinstead and Lewes, only around 7,000 people lived in the area served by the route (with Barcombe the only station located near the centre of a village), the enquiry report concluded that the line could not be regarded as a suitable relief line for London trains, and maintained that 'though the buses did not give services in the immediate vicinity of the stations equal to or as convenient as that provided by the trains, they formed an adequate network of country services.'[28] *The Times* sounded the death-knell of the line as follows:

> 'The "Bluebell Line", which provides a service of trains between Lewes and East Grinstead, will close down on March 17 … The committee state in their report that the withdrawal of the service would be in the public interest. It is clear, they add, that a railway which loses at least £33,000 annually … cannot be kept open in the public interest unless there is some major overriding consideration of national policy which can be satisfied only by keeping the railway running. They heard no evidence of any such overriding circumstance in this case.'[29]

(Readers will note that, unlike the annual loss of £59,000 stated by the BTC in 1954, the line was now only losing £33,000 a year. This apparent improvement was due to the greatly reduced level of service provided since the enforced reopening in 1956.)

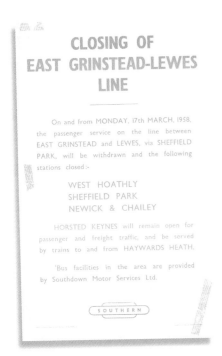

CLOSING OF
EAST GRINSTEAD-LEWES
LINE

On and from MONDAY, 17th MARCH, 1958, the passenger service on the line between EAST GRINSTEAD and LEWES, via SHEFFIELD PARK, will be withdrawn and the following stations closed:-

WEST HOATHLY
SHEFFIELD PARK
NEWICK & CHAILEY

HORSTED KEYNES will remain open for passenger and freight traffic, and be served by trains to and from HAYWARDS HEATH.

'Bus facilities in the area are provided by Southdown Motor Services Ltd.

SOUTHERN

ABOVE LEFT The British Railways poster announcing the withdrawal of all services between East Grinstead and Lewes, which would take place on **Monday 17 March 1958.** *Bluebell Railway Museum Archive*

ABOVE RIGHT The British Transport Commission closed the East Grinstead to Lewes line for the second, and final, time on Sunday 16 March 1958. A six-coach formation operated throughout the day, with the first two return journeys being operated by BR Standard Class 4MT No 80011, as seen here at Sheffield Park with the 12.28pm East Grinstead to Lewes train. *John Scrace, Bluebell Railway Museum Archive*

Where was Dr Beeching?

The name of Dr Richard (later Lord) Beeching is so synonymous with the widespread post-war closure of British railway lines that some readers may be surprised by his absence from this account of the fight to close the Bluebell line and will be asking where he was and what he was doing while these events were occurring. The answer to where he was is that he was happily living at the northern end of the route in his house at East Grinstead. The answer to what he was doing at the time is that he was working for ICI. Beeching had no involvement with the British Transport Commission until 1959 and was not appointed as Chairman of the BTC until as late as 1961. Sadly, by then the Bluebell line, like a surprisingly large number of branch lines, had become so unremunerative that it did not even survive long enough to fall victim to Beeching's axe.

In 1963, by which time the preserved Bluebell Railway was in its fourth year of operation, Beeching became Chairman of the newly created British Railways Board, successor to the BTC. That year would see the closure of the Ardingly branch and the publication of the infamous 'Beeching report', *The Reshaping of*

ABOVE The final two return journeys over the Lewes to East Grinstead line were handled by BR Standard Class 4MT No 80145, the last ever engine to be built at Brighton Works. Seen here at Horsted Keynes, the engine pauses to take water with the final northbound service, the 3.30pm from Lewes to East Grinstead. Horsted Keynes was noted for its unreliable water supply, hence the sign advising locomotive crews to take water only 'when absolutely necessary'. *Bluebell Railway Museum Archive*

Britain's Railways, announcing, among many other route closures, the forthcoming demise of the earliest railway to serve East Grinstead, the route from Tunbridge Wells, as well as its continuation west to Three Bridges. (In fact, the only railway line from East Grinstead to remain open by the end of the decade was the route north towards London, the very line on which Beeching was a regular commuter.) It is only to be wondered what Beeching had made of the earlier futile campaign to save the local Lewes to East Grinstead line in the 1950s.

A section of the former railway from East Grinstead to Tunbridge Wells would eventually be obliterated by the construction of the East Grinstead inner relief road, which opened in 1978. The road was named Beeching Way, after the title Beeching Cut was allegedly rejected.

The last day

The last day of operation between Lewes and East Grinstead fell on Sunday 16 March 1958 and, unlike the quiet demise of 1955, this time the passing of the now-famous line was marked with a blaze of attention from public, media and enthusiasts alike. Five hundred passengers were carried on the Saturday, with well over twice that number present for the final day. Local and national newspapers were present to record the event, as well as cameras from both the BBC and ITN.

A rake of six carriages operated throughout the day, replacing the normal single-coach formation; the first two return journeys were operated by Class 4 2-6-4T No 80011. For the third return journey an immaculate No 80154 was rostered to take over, being the last locomotive to be built at Brighton Works. For the final trip of the day, the late-running 4.28pm departure from East Grinstead, a further three coaches were added to the formation and No 80154 was fitted with a special 'Bluebell' headboard, featuring a large 'V' symbol emblazoned with a hand-painted bluebell and garlanded with flowers. Reported the next day's *Times*:

'East Grinstead, March 16
The "bluebell line", the Sussex branch railway that has linked East Grinstead with Lewes, died officially this afternoon when a nine-coach train hauled by a standard tank engine pulled out of East Grinstead at 4.48pm… At each of the six intermediate stations between East Grinstead and Lewes to-day crowds flocked to see the last train go through, and at East Grinstead station there were more than 1,000 people on the platform. Twice during the hour trip to Lewes the train had to stop when over-enthusiastic passengers had applied the brake in the train.'[30]

BELOW With the formation strengthened to nine coaches, BR Standard 4MT No 80145 passes near Barcombe with the final passenger train over the Lewes to East Grinstead line, the late-running 4.28pm East Grinstead to Lewes service. The V-shaped headboard carries a hand-painted bluebell and is garlanded with flowers. *J. H. W. Kent, Bluebell Railway Museum Archive*

LEFT The last rites. The Station Master of Lewes, Mr J. H. Barnwell, poses with members of his staff alongside No 80145 upon the arrival of the final train from East Grinstead on 16 March 1958. *Bluebell Railway Museum Archive*

Some 870 passengers were officially recorded as travelling on the final run, although unofficial estimates suggest that as many as 1,000 may have been on board by the time the train arrived at Lewes an hour later. Among them were 83-year-old Kate Longley, who had ridden on the first service over the LEGR in 1882, and 90-year-old Charles Newnham, who as a boy had worked on the construction of the line.

Such was the fame of the line by now that even the *Washington Post* carried the story, informing its readers that 'The Bluebell and Primrose Railroad made its last run today,

victim of a Government white paper, a special act of Parliament and the age of speed.'[31] The article is notable for including the anecdote that 'Passengers always said the train went so slow they could lean out and pick bluebells and primroses on the trackside', but also for a number of factual inaccuracies. The 17-mile line was claimed to be the 'smallest branch line in England' (!) while of the final train the paper reported that 'the old Bluebell and Primrose pulled out of East Grinstead station for the scheduled 45-minute last run exactly on time.' (In reality it was 20 minutes late.)

The end of the line?

Sunday 16 March 1958 had marked the end of regular services on the Lewes to East Grinstead line, but, for the northern section at least, it was not quite the end. With the Ardingly branch to Horsted Keynes still very much open, the route from Horsted Keynes to East Grinstead continued to be maintained

ABOVE Maunsell 'N' Class No 31815 passes through Ardingly with a southbound Lingfield to Brighton 'Race Special' in 1951. These specials would continue to operate via the Ardingly branch and over the Horsted Keynes to East Grinstead section until October 1960, 2½ years after the route north of Horsted Keynes had been closed to regular passenger traffic. *Bluebell Railway Museum Archive*

LEFT At the head of one of the very many trains that traversed the northern section of the Lewes to East Grinstead line during the 2½-year period after its formal closure, BR Standard tank Class 4MT No 80138 (strangely devoid of a smokebox numberplate) heads south through Kingscote with a train of condemned wagons bound for Lancing in March 1960. *Derek Cross, Bluebell Railway Museum Archive*

on a 'care and maintenance' basis (possibly pending a future decision on electrification), allowing the operation of occasional special trains via East Grinstead-Horsted Keynes-Haywards Heath for the time being. Two Sunday School excursions operated over the line in June 1958, while race specials from Brighton to Lingfield racetrack continued to operate, the earliest appearing on the line within a few days of the closure date having passed. Special ramblers' excursions, often organised by the Ramblers' Association, had been associated with the line since the 1930s, and these too continued to run over the northern section after the cessation of regular services. The first post-closure ramblers' special was the 'Bluebell special', a privately organised tour that departed from Greenford in Middlesex behind celebrity GWR loco No 3440 *City of Truro* on 11 May 1958. Faced with clearance restrictions south of East Grinstead, the 'City' was replaced by 'K' Class No 32342, which took the train forward to its advertised destinations of Horsted Keynes and Ardingly. Further ramblers' specials ran over the line in December 1958 and September 1959, on these occasions hauled by Bulleid 'Pacifics', while 12 July 1959 offered a taste of things to come when the northern section of the line was traversed by the first

BELOW Another trainload of condemned wagons en route for Lancing is seen this time seen crossing Imberhorne Viaduct in April 1960. The locomotive is Maunsell 'U1' Class 2-6-0 No 31890. *Derek Cross, Bluebell Railway Museum Archive*

railtour organised by the newly formed Bluebell Railway Preservation Society (BRPS).

From 14 July 1959 the up line north of Horsted Keynes was demoted to a siding for the storage of condemned wagons, and from then on all trains were routed via the former down line. More than 1,200 wagons were delivered by 32 trains in just over a month, only to be removed again during 1959-60. Taking into account tunnel inspection trains, weedkilling trains, empty coaching stock workings and diverted newspaper trains, it is reckoned that by the end of 1959 more than 160 separate workings had been made over the line north of Horsted Keynes since its formal closure.

The last passenger service over the northern section of the Bluebell line in the 20th century was a Lingfield race special headed by Fairburn 2-6-4T No 42067 on Thursday 1 October 1959. After that date all railtours and ramblers' specials were routed via the Ardingly branch – at least while it remained open. The final recorded BR-owned locomotive to appear north of Horsted Keynes was 'Q' Class No 30544, which worked a ballast train on 9 December 1960.

The birth of the heritage railway movement

On 18 March 1959 the following announcement appeared in the Personal adverts of *The Times*:

BLUEBELL LINE. – Join determined and enthusiastic Society formed to re-open line. Write enclosing stamped addressed envelope to: Lewes-East Grinstead Railway Preservation Society, 97, Leylands Road, Burgess Hill.'[32]

In 21st-century Britain the heritage railway movement is a major contributor to the leisure industry, but in the 1950s the situation was very different – railway preservation was in its infancy and the success of this 'determined and enthusiastic Society' would have been very much an unknown quantity.

It was only eight years earlier, in 1951, that the Talyllyn Railway in mid-Wales had become the very first preserved railway in the world when a similar group of enthusiastic volunteers had successfully taken over the running of the line. In 1954 another group of enthusiasts took control of the Ffestiniog Railway, commencing passenger services in 1955. In that same year the Bluebell line closed for the first time. Had the line remained closed, and had the BTC dismantled the infrastructure shortly afterwards, it seems highly likely that no part of the route would ever have reopened. As it was, the time and publicity bought by Madge Bessemer's temporarily successful campaign to reopen the line, coupled with the successful examples set by the Talyllyn and Ffestiniog lines, had given enthusiasts cause to think that maybe the Bluebell could be preserved for future generations as well.

However, the Talyllyn and Ffestiniog railways were both a very different proposition from the Bluebell line. Both were able to offer day-trippers and tourists the almost unique opportunity of riding a quaint narrow-gauge railway through the dramatic Welsh countryside, offering scenic views of hills, valleys and mountains; and both had termini by the Cambrian coast. By contrast, the Bluebell, for all the attractive views that rural Sussex had to offer, was just one of many standard-gauge branch lines in the English Home Counties. Steam-operated branch lines, and even main lines, were still the norm across most of the United Kingdom in 1959. Within a decade the railway scene would change beyond recognition, but in this pre-Beeching and largely pre-modernisation age steam was still king. British Railways was at this date still building steam locomotives (the final new BR steam loco, No 92220 *Evening Star*, would not emerge from Swindon Works until the following year). Even on the Southern Region, where the electrified third-rail network had been expanding for decades, one did not have to travel far to find rural branch lines operated by steam (the electrified Ardingly branch was very much the exception in this case). The question of whether anyone would take a special day trip to travel in antiquated carriages behind a steam locomotive on a standard-gauge preserved railway when they could probably have the same experience on their own local British Railways line was still an unknown quantity. The Bluebell Railway Preservation Society was about to try and find out the answer.

The birth of the Bluebell Railway

The advert that appeared in the 'Personal' column of *The Times* on 18 March had come three days after the founding of what was initially called the 'Lewes to East Grinstead Railway Preservation Society'. Held at the Church Lads' Brigade Hall in Haywards Heath, the inaugural meeting had been called by four young men, Chris Campbell, David Dallimore, Martin Eastland and Alan Sturt, most of whom were still students. Recognising their youth, the four pioneers arranged for a local enthusiast, Bernard Holden, to chair the initial meeting. Holden himself was a lifelong railwayman and had actually been born in Barcombe station, where his father had been station master in the early years of the 20th century. Involved from the beginning, he would ultimately go on to become a long-serving President of the BRPS until his death, aged 104, in 2012.

One hundred and fifty individuals, including Madge Bessemer[33], attended the meeting on 15 March at which the preservation society came into being with the initial aim of acquiring and operating the entire line from Lewes to East Grinstead. Media interest in the Bluebell line continued, with the meeting reported in the national press. Stated *The Guardian*:

'Mr Alan Sturt, a Brighton economics student, told the society's first meeting ... that the British Transport Commission's figure for the purchase of the line was about £40,000, but it was hoped to persuade it to lease the line to the society. It was also hoped to buy a disused GWR diesel railcar and run it between Horsted Keynes and Sheffield Park – about four and a half miles – during the summer season for a start.'[34]

The mention here of operating an ex-GWR railcar is particularly interesting, as in 1959 this would almost certainly not have been considered a heritage attraction. For some years anti-closure protestors had advocated that BR experiment with running lightweight diesel units on the line as a cost-saving measure. Its inclusion here suggests that at this stage the new preservation society harboured ambitions of operating at least part of the route as a cost-effective public service – something that the BTC had never succeeded in doing (although admittedly it might not have been trying very hard) – rather than a purely steam-operated tourist attraction.

By the time of a further meeting in June 1959 a group from the society had already met with the BTC (which had initially dismissed the delegation as little more than a group of 'schoolboys'!) and had been forced to adapt its aims to allow for what was now known to be realistic. The BTC it seemed was actually asking the sum of £75,000 to purchase the section of line from Culver Junction to within a few hundred yards south of Horsted Keynes station. There seemed little possibility that through running would ever be allowed over BR tracks into Lewes, and the still-mothballed section of line from Horsted Keynes to East Grinstead appeared not to be up for sale either – even if the money had been available, which it certainly was not. Faced with the seeming impossibility of ever raising £75,000, and the fact that BR was keen to proceed with lifting the tracks on the southern section of the route, the society reluctantly decided to concentrate its efforts on preserving just the Sheffield Park to Horsted Keynes section, for which the BTC was asking a mere £34,000. (Even the raising of this sum was by no means an easy target for a society that at this stage was reported to have a total of £89 5s in its funds.[35]) No further mention of diesel railcars was made, and from this point on the intention was to create a steam-operated heritage railway, with its base at Sheffield Park. It was also now that the Lewes to East Grinstead Railway Preservation Society became the Bluebell Railway Preservation Society, perhaps in recognition of the fact that neither Lewes nor East Grinstead seemed attainable goals for the society, but also more practically the fact that the 'Bluebell line' was already nationally famous and hence a tourist attraction in the making.

Why preserve Sheffield Park to Horsted Keynes?

The decision of the BRPS to concentrate its efforts on a section of line in the middle of the route, between two stations that were, frankly, in the middle of nowhere, might at first seem odd (leaving aside the fact that the members' hands were probably tied by the machinations of the BTC anyway). However, it was a sound decision. The landscape gardens at Sheffield Park, laid out by 'Capability' Brown in the 18th century and acquired by the National Trust in 1954, were already, and continue to be, a tourist attraction in their own right, and thus likely to bring additional visitors to the new railway. Meanwhile, with access to both Lewes and East Grinstead denied to the preservationists, the advantage of Horsted Keynes was that it provided a direct link to the national railway network – at least for as long as the Ardingly branch remained open. This must have seemed a vital link at the time for not only did it allow for potential visitors to arrive by train (even if the two railways were not initially allowed to share the same station) but it also provided a physical link for trains to pass from the national system to the Bluebell Railway. For the next few years both railtours and newly acquired rolling stock were able to arrive via the Ardingly branch onto Bluebell metals at Horsted Keynes. With this connection in place, the Sheffield Park to Horsted Keynes section of line must have seemed like a very good choice indeed.

Progress

On 12 July 1959 the first railtour organised by the fledgling preservation society started at Tonbridge and ran to Eridge via East Grinstead, Horsted Keynes, Haywards Heath, Keymer Junction and Lewes. The only such BRPS tour to traverse the northern section of the line (in future all such tours would arrive via the Ardingly branch), the special paused at Horsted Keynes where the chairman of the society addressed around 300 passengers from a signal gantry. This was followed on 27 September by a rally at Sheffield Park station, where the BRPS had already set up its base, at which a pump trolley was used to demonstrate the operation of the recently reinstated signalling. On this occasion a ramblers' special operated down the northern section of the line en route for Ardingly and a carriage was reserved for BRPS members, who alighted at Horsted Keynes to catch a bus service to Sheffield Park. The rally was well attended with around 500 supporters, not all of them members, present at Sheffield Park. Reporting the event, *The Guardian* noted that 'it was hoped that trips from Sheffield Park to Horsted Keynes would be available to the public in May at a return fare of 2s 6d.'[36] *The Times* noted that 'The society at present had 400 members and it was hoped to increase this to 1,000.'[37]

Throughout this period negotiations with the BTC continued but, despite the optimism expressed at the September rally, it was becoming increasingly clear that the full sum of £34,000 was not going to be available any time soon. In lieu of this, on Christmas Eve 1959 the BTC offered a five-year lease on the Sheffield Park to Horsted Keynes line. The details of the agreement were revealed at a BRPS meeting held at Brighton Pavilion on 19 February 1960 and reported by *The Times* the following day:

> 'Backers of the "Bluebell" railway … will have to pay £2,250 a year to keep the line open, and 2,000 members will be needed, a meeting of 200 railway enthusiasts was told in Brighton last night. At present there are 600 members of the Bluebell Railway Preservation Society, who called the meeting to give the public facts and figures about their negotiations with the British Transport Commission to take the line over. […] In December the society … was granted a five-year lease to operate the line, but the lease will not become operative until a light railway order is granted. At the end of five years the society will be given the option to purchase.'[38]

Quoting the society's Chief Engineer, the article reported that 'an engine and rolling stock would be bought as soon as the lease was signed', while one of the trustees advised that '10,000 man-hours a year would be needed to keep the line open.'

Also required to legally operate the line would be a limited company, and five days later a further article in *The Times* announced that 'A company, Bluebell Railway Ltd, has been registered with a nominal capital of £100 in £1 shares to acquire the track between East Grinstead and Lewes, Sussex.'[39] There was still much to be done before the line could re-open – rolling stock would need to be acquired, a halt needed to be constructed at Horsted Keynes (where Bluebell trains were to terminate a few hundred yards south of the BR station), and a loco shed and inspection pit needed to be built at Sheffield Park – but slowly the preservation dream was turning into reality.

Rolling stock

In May 1960 the BRPS finally acquired its first locomotive. Reported *The Guardian*:

> 'The engine, Terrier 32655 (ex 655 Stepney), has been bought from the British Transport Commission and should arrive by the middle of this month, together with two coaches. The society is hoping to run trains from the middle of July and negotiations are in hand for a second engine, "as in the early stages of operation the train will require an engine at both ends".'[40]

The need to operate with an engine at each end of the train referred to the fact that the primitive 'Bluebell Halt' station

BELOW A major goal was achieved on 17 May 1960 when the Bluebell Railway took delivery of its first rolling stock. Ex-LBSCR 'Terrier' No 55 *Stepney*, having arrived under its own steam from Brighton, departs from Horsted Keynes for Sheffield Park with coaches Nos S6575 and S320 in tow. *Bluebell Railway Museum Archive*

under its own power on 17 May 1960, and the need for a second loco was addressed shortly after with the coming of ex-SECR 'P' Class No 323 on 27 June. In truth, most BRPS members at the time would probably have preferred another ex-LBSCR loco – specifically another Class 'A1X' like *Stepney* – but BR had no more to spare at the time and the 0-6-0T 'P' Class probably suited the Bluebell's operating needs in 1960 just as well as a 'Terrier'. (Unlike today, the Bluebell Railway of 1960 was very much a 'small engine' line.) Certainly as far as most non-enthusiast visitors were concerned one pre-Grouping 0-6-0 tank engine would probably look very much like another anyway.

So, by the end of May 1960 the Bluebell Railway had possession of 4½ miles of railway line, one fully restored Victorian station, two hastily constructed wooden halts (in addition to 'Bluebell Halt' at Horsted Keynes, another had been constructed part way along the line at Freshfield), two operational locomotives and two passenger coaches. All four vehicles would be required to run in each train, but provided that 100% availability could be ensured the BRPS had everything it needed to run a railway. All that was missing was a Light Railway Order, and to acquire that a Ministry of Transport inspection would need to be carried out, just as it had been in 1882.

Inspection

The inspection was finally carried out by Colonel J. R. H. Robertson on 9 July 1960, a day that one of the Bluebell Railway's directors, Captain Peter Manisty RN (Retd) referred to as 'probably the most important day in our life'. Capt Manisty was quoted in *The Observer*, in an article that described the inspection in detail:

'Col Robertson tested the signals and the signal man… He watched two tank engines steam down and couple up, and bent low to view this manoeuvre, expertly

ABOVE Bluebell Halt is under construction to the south of Horsted Keynes during 1960. The Bluebell Railway would not gain full regular access to Horsted Keynes BR station until the 1962 running season. *K. D. Chown, Bluebell Railway Museum Archive*

RIGHT The Bluebell Railway's entire locomotive fleet for the 1960 operating season comprised 'Terrier' No 55 *Stepney* and 'P' Class No 323 *Bluebell*. Both locomotives would be required to operate every service, owing to the lack of run-round facilities at the northern end of the line. *K. D. Chown, Bluebell Railway Museum Archive*

under construction to the south of BR's Horsted Keynes station was to have no run-round facilities. The article also noted that Sheffield Park station had already been restored and that 'a Ministry of Transport inspector is to make what the society hopes will be a final inspection of the line in June.'

The two coaches acquired with *Stepney* were LSWR 3rd Class vehicle No S320 and 1929 Southern Railway Maunsell Brake Composite No S6575; for the 1960 operating season these were to form the Bluebell's entire carriage fleet. *Stepney* arrived via the Ardingly branch, with the two carriages in tow,

ABOVE Prior to opening to the public, the first 'passenger' train on the preserved Bluebell Railway was recorded by photographer Roger Lunn on 30 July 1960. Here the train, consisting of 'Terrier' No 55 *Stepney*, coach No S320 and 'P' Class No 323 *Bluebell*, arrives back at Sheffield Park from Bluebell Halt. Note the open ground frame on Platform 1, at this stage still surrounded only by a fence. *Roger Lunn, Bluebell Railway Museum Archive*

RIGHT 'P' Class No 323 is formally christened *Bluebell* by the breaking of a bottle of champagne by Mrs Elizabeth Kimmins prior to the departure of the very first timetabled Bluebell Railway service on 7 August 1960. *Bluebell Railway Museum Archive*

performed… Putting on a black oilskin, the colonel rode on the footplate to get the feel of the line, to inspect features (there are 65 bridges and culverts) and to see if the driver could drive. (The drivers can drive. They are retired British Railways drivers, who have eagerly taken the chance to get back to their old love, steam.)

The result of to-day's inspection will be known in a week. The omens are good. If all is well, the line opens on August 7 – with the unpaid operating staff in period uniforms. Sheffield Park to Horsted Keynes return (with entrance to the railway museum) will cost 2s 6d second class, 3s 6d first, and the round trip takes 50 minutes.'[41]

Opening

The omens were good. The inspection was passed with flying colours and, as predicted, the new Bluebell Railway was formally opened on 7 August 1960. More than 2,000 people, including many BRPS members in Victorian dress, were admitted to witness the opening ceremony at 3pm, at which playwright Anthony Kimmins, another retired naval captain, gave a short speech before his wife broke a bottle of champagne over 'P' Class No 323, newly adorned with the name *Bluebell*. Other invited guests included 92-year-old Mrs Sarah Funnell of Barcombe,

ABOVE Crowds line the platforms (and, in some cases, stand on the tracks!) as Stroudley 'Terrier' No 55 *Stepney* prepares to depart from Sheffield Park on the Bluebell Railway's opening day. 'P' Class No 323 *Bluebell* is on the rear of the two-coach train. Note the film cameraman balanced on the platform canopy. *Bluebell Railway Museum Archive*

who had witnessed the construction of the line, and Miss Kate Longley, aged 84, who had travelled on both the first LEGR service in 1882 and the final BR train in 1958. A brass band played, the engines' bunkers sported white-painted coal, and by the end of the first day more than 900 fare-paying passengers had been carried. Once again, the Bluebell attracted a blaze of national, and international, media attention, *The Baltimore Sun* wryly commenting: 'The line has little point in the transportation scheme of things but it's a whale of a lot of fun.'[42]

The Bluebell Railway was not quite the first standard-gauge preserved railway in Britain; that honour had already been taken by the Middleton Railway, which had reopened as a preserved line in June 1960. However, the Middleton was primarily a freight line and would not begin regular passenger services for another nine years, meaning that the Bluebell was undoubtedly the first standard-gauge preserved passenger railway in Britain. Two years after the final BR train had departed from East Grinstead for Lewes, a section of the old LEGR was open for business again and a small but determined group of volunteers had achieved a major landmark in British railway history.

CHAPTER EIGHT

· ·

Preservation – the early years

The Bluebell Railway's first season of operation was to prove a great success, exceeding the expectations of its founders, yet the future of the new railway was by no means guaranteed. The railway still only owned two coaches and two locomotives – the absolute minimum needed to operate the service – making the acquisition of further stock an urgent requirement.

BLUEBELL RAILWAY

SHEFFIELD
PARK

HORSTED
KEYNES

Through five miles of Glorious Sussex Scenery and
connecting at Horsted Keynes with British Railways.

Museum of Historic Railway Relics and Models. Refreshment Rooms & Tea Garden, together with excellent parking facilities at Sheffield Park Station the Headquarters of the Bluebell Railway Preservation Society.

COME AND TRAVEL ON THIS FAMOUS LINE
WITH VINTAGE ENGINES AND COACHES.

TIMETABLE 1962

Every SATURDAY and SUNDAY from 31st March to 28th October.
EASTER MONDAY 23rd April and WHIT MONDAY 11th June.
WEDNESDAY 16th May and every WEDNESDAY from 6th June to 12th September inclusive.
DAILY from 21st July to 2nd September inclusive.

UP.		a.m.	p.m.	p.m.	p.m.	p.m.	p.m.	p.m.
Sheffield Park	dep.	11.50	1.50	2.50	3.50	4.42	5.50	6.50
Freshfield	arr.	11.58	1.58	2.58	3.58	4.50	5.58	6.58
Holywell (Waterworks)	arr.	12.3	2.3	3.3	4.3	4.55	6.3	7.3
Bluebell Halt	arr.	12.6	2.6	3.6	4.6	5.0	6.6	7.6
Horsted Keynes (S.R.)	arr.	12.10	2.10	3.10	4.10	5.2	6.10	7.10
Horsted Keynes (S.R.) To Haywards Heath and beyond	dep.	12.16d	2.16d	3.16s	4.16d	5.8ss	6.16d	7.23ss
DOWN.		a.m.	p.m.	p.m.	p.m.	p.m.	p.m.	p.m.
Horsted Keynes (S.R.) from Haywards Heath	arr.	11.13d	12.14d	2.13d	3.13ss	4.13d	5.3ss	6.14d	7.5ss
Horsted Keynes (S.R.)	dep.	11.30	12.30	2.30	3.30	4.18	5.30	6.30	7.15
Bluebell Halt	dep.	11.33	12.33	2.33	3.33	4.30	5.43	6.33	7.17
Holywell (Waterworks)	dep.	11.36	12.36	2.36	3.36	4.34	5.36	6.36	7.31
Freshfield	dep.	11.51	12.51	2.51	3.51	4.39	5.21	6.51	7.26
Sheffield Park	arr.	11.57	12.57	2.57	3.57	4.35	5.27	6.57	7.32

NOTES: Applicable to BRITISH RAILWAYS (SOUTHERN REGION) train times at HORSTED KEYNES. d—Daily. ss—Not Sundays. ss—Not Saturdays or Sundays.

FARE. 2/6d. Return 2nd Class. 3/6d. 1st Class. (Singles also available). Children under 14 half-fare
Parties at reduced rates. Write to General Manager, Bluebell Railway, Sheffield Park Station, Uckfield,
Sussex, or ring Newick 370.

Through Combined Southern/Bluebell Line cheap tickets via Horsted Keynes are obtainable from Victoria, London Bridge, Clapham Junction,
E. Croydon, Epsom, Sutton, Eastbourne, Brighton and many other stations.

ENQUIRE AT YOUR LOCAL STATION

Printed by TUCKER & SELLS LTD., 11 LEDINGTON St., LONDON, S.E.1.

Maintenance facilities and covered accommodation for rolling stock were clearly inadequate, bordering on the non-existent, and the BRPS did not even own the track over which it was operating. Instead, an annual lease fee was being paid to British Railways for the use of the line, a lease that was itself due to expire in five years. As well as all this, it was becoming increasingly obvious that the Ardingly branch was living on borrowed time; would the new railway even be able to survive without this link to the national network? The next few years would be crucial in securing the long-term survival of the Bluebell Railway.

The first season

Having opened for traffic on 7 August 1960, by the time the first season drew to a close in October the initial success of the new railway was clear to see. Noted *The Times*:

> 'In the two months since the Bluebell line from Horsted Keynes to Sheffield Park, Sussex, was reopened 12,000 passengers have been carried, and gross receipts from all sources have exceeded £2,000. Membership of the Bluebell Railway Preservation Society is now more than 1,500. The line closes for the winter at the end of this month.'[43]

Nothing succeeds like success, and at the BRPS's annual meeting, held in Haywards Heath on 4 December, it was announced that the final total of passengers carried during the 1960 operating season was 15,000, with receipts from fares

LEFT An early Bluebell Railway timetable poster from 1962 – a year in which the 5-mile line could boast of no fewer than five different stations! Holywell Halt was enjoying its only year in use, while the continued inclusion of Bluebell Halt in the timetable at this date meant that passengers had the luxury of choosing which side of the road they wished to leave the train at Horsted Keynes. The interchange with BR at Horsted Keynes is advertised, but the much greater emphasis on the 'excellent parking facilities at Sheffield Park' suggests that few passengers were arriving via the Ardingly branch. The artwork shows No 323 *Bluebell*, although apparently in a fictitious green livery.
Bluebell Railway Museum Archive

TOP The Bluebell Railway's only train in 1960 comprised 'Terrier' No 55 *Stepney* (on the left, facing Horsted Keynes), LSWR 3rd Class No S320, Maunsell Brake Composite No S6575, and 'P' Class No 323 *Bluebell* (facing Sheffield Park). With no other vehicles available and each train required to be top-and-tailed, this was literally the formation of every single train. *Mike Esau, Bluebell Railway Museum Archive*

ABOVE This rare shot from March 1961 shows newly arrived ex-SECR 'P' Class No 27, on the right, carrying unlined black livery and before receiving the name *Primrose*. On the left No 323 *Bluebell* demonstrates what No 27 will shortly look like. *K. D. Chown, Bluebell Railway Museum Archive*

alone amounting to £1,136 – impressive figures considering that the line had only been open for two months and then only at weekends. As reported in *The Times*, Horace May, the line's General Manager, stated that the 1961 operating season would begin on 1 April and that 'Among the society's urgent requirements was a third passenger engine.'[44]

This requirement certainly was urgent; the continued absence of run-round facilities at the northern end of the line meant that two engines were still required to operate every train – and two engines were all the railway possessed at that time. Finally the need was met in March 1961 with the arrival of a second ex-SECR 'P' Class tank engine, No 27, which, following the example set by its sister *Bluebell*, quickly acquired the name *Primrose*.

The question of liveries

One need only look at the heated debates in recent years surrounding the 'correct' livery for the *Flying Scotsman* to know that few subjects arouse the passion of railway enthusiasts as much as that of liveries. The arrival of *Primrose* in 1961 provides an opportunity to look at the early livery policies of the Bluebell Railway. For many decades now almost all heritage organisations, including the Bluebell, have adhered to an unwritten rule that where at all possible rolling stock, especially locomotives, should be restored in historically correct liveries. However, in 1960 the rules for heritage railways had yet to be established and, faced with a blank page, the Bluebell initially embarked upon a slightly different policy.

When the Bluebell Railway first opened to paying passengers in 1960 both of its locomotives were painted in lined black liveries – although in truth this was largely because both locos had been delivered from BR in unlined black, and the Bluebell volunteers had simply not had the time or facilities for a full repaint before opening day. Both engines had been renumbered with their original pre-Grouping numbers, 55 for the 'A1X' 'Terrier', which also regained its original name *Stepney*, and 323 for the 'P' Class. The newly renumbered 323, which had never before carried a name, was now christened *Bluebell* – making it something of a flagship for the railway (although fans of *Stepney* might disagree!). Unlike the locomotives, the railway's two carriages had received a full repaint and debuted in a new all over 'Bluebell blue' livery (not wholly unlike the all-over blue livery that British Rail would adopt for its own suburban stock from the mid-'60s onwards). The winter of 1960/61 saw the first shift towards historical liveries when *Stepney* was repainted in the open air to her original 'Stroudley's Improved Engine Green' livery, yet the arrival of *Primrose* in 1961 again saw a combination of lined black livery, pre-Grouping number and a new name. Later that year ex-LSWR Adams 'Radial' tank No 488 would become the first unnamed Bluebell engine, entering straight into service still

TOP LEFT Over the winter of 1960/61 'Terrier' No 55 *Stepney* was repainted into full Stroudley's Improved Engine Green livery – becoming the first Bluebell locomotive to receive a historically accurate livery. An almost total lack of covered accommodation meant that all locomotive repaints were carried out in the open air at this time. *Bluebell Railway Museum Archive*

TOP RIGHT 'P' Class No 323 *Bluebell* displays its original Bluebell Railway livery at Sheffield Park circa 1962. Behind it can be seen Adams 'Radial' tank No 488, 'Terrier' No 55 *Stepney* (with white-painted coal in her bunker), and ex-North London Railway tank No 2650. *Kevin Robertson*

ABOVE Ex-LBSCR 'E4' Class No 473 stands at Sheffield Park at the head of the ex-London Transport 'Chesham' set, apparently in the autumn of 1962. Note that the loco has regained its pre-Grouping number but retains BR livery albeit with the crest painted out; over the winter of 1962/63 No 473 was restored to full LBSCR livery as *Birch Grove*. *Kevin Robertson*

RIGHT 'Terrier' No 72 *Fenchurch* braves the winter snow at Horsted Keynes as it runs round its train prior to hauling it back to Sheffield Park on 29 November 1969. At least one of the carriages in the background carries 'Bluebell blue' livery. *Len Walton*

carrying full BR lined-black livery, with only the change to a pre-Grouping number to distinguish it from its previous role.

A 1966 guidebook includes a table of all actual and intended liveries carried by Bluebell locomotives and coaches at the time, providing a neat snapshot of the Bluebell's livery policy in the mid-1960s.[45] By this time almost the entire locomotive fleet was carrying historically correct, largely pre-Grouping, liveries. The one non-historical livery in 1966 was *Bluebell* itself, which in that year lost its black livery in favour of 'Bluebell' blue. Retaining her eponymous name (her sister *Primrose* had lost her name when restored to SECR livery in 1963), *Bluebell* has carried versions of this blue livery ever since, the only loco to do so, reinforcing her status as a flagship loco for the railway.

The livery policy for coaching stock in the mid-'60s is more confusing. While both of the original two Bluebell carriages were 'scheduled' in the guidebook to lose their blue livery for historically correct liveries, two other carriages were due to receive 'Bluebell Company Blue'. Other carriages listed in the guidebook carried, or were scheduled to carry, historically correct liveries, but 'Bluebell blue' would continue to be present on some coaches for the remainder of the decade.

Noticeably absent from the Bluebell's liveries in the mid-'60s were any representatives from the British Railways era – perhaps not surprising considering that BR had expended so much effort in running down and closing the Lewes to East Grinstead line in the previous decade, and was at that very moment working to eliminate steam from the whole of the national network. More surprising perhaps was the absence, save for one carriage, of any livery from the Southern Railway era. A 1970 Bluebell publication describes the policy of the time as being 'to restore locomotives to their original company livery'[46]. In understanding this it is worth remembering that in the 1960s enthusiasts as young as their mid-40s would have been able to remember the liveries of the pre-Grouping era from their own childhood. Today, 50 years later, those enthusiasts still old enough to remember the steam era go misty-eyed at the sight of the liveries of the BR era – the liveries they remember from their youth – and these are now the liveries seemingly favoured by many heritage railways and model railway manufacturers. The Bluebell Railway of the 21st century features rolling stock and liveries from all eras up to and including the end of the BR steam era, but visitors today can still be guaranteed the site of locomotives in the elaborately lined liveries of the pre-Grouping companies.

New arrivals

When the Bluebell Railway reopened for its second season in April 1961 the first train was powered by all three locomotives, *Stepney* and *Primrose* at the front, and *Bluebell* bringing up the rear, behind four newly acquired passenger carriages.

These new coaches were ex-Metropolitan Railway Ashbury carriages built between 1898 and 1900. Originally used for steam haulage, they had been converted for electric multiple unit duties in the early 20th century; any survivors were then converted back to steam-hauled stock in 1940 for use on London Transport's Chesham branch. Made redundant by electrification in 1960, the coaches arrived on the Bluebell in

BELOW Ex-SECR 'P' Class No 323 *Bluebell* arrives at Sheffield Park with a down train on 1 April 1961, the first day of the 1961 operating season. The coaches are the newly arrived 'Chesham' set, while at the rear of the train will be either *Stepney* or *Primrose*, or possibly both. *Bluebell Railway Museum Archive*

ABOVE Ex-LSWR Adams 'Radial' 0-4-4T No 488, already shorn of its BR identity and crest, passes through Ardingly station under its own steam en route to the Bluebell Railway in July 1961. This was the normal way for new stock to arrive at the Bluebell until the electrified branch was lifted in 1964. *Bluebell Railway Museum Archive*

March 1961, reportedly for £65 each, and instantly trebled the size of the infant railway's carriage fleet. Forming the backbone of the Bluebell's passenger fleet for much of the 1960s, by the middle of the decade they were considered to be probably the oldest standard-gauge carriages still in UK passenger service.

The entry into service of *Primrose* had provided the Bluebell with its much-needed third locomotive, but the railway still had its sights set upon expanding its fleet and a fourth locomotive was to arrive later in the year. This was Adams 'Radial' tank No 30583, swiftly renumbered to its original identity of 488, which had been targeted as much for its historical value as for its operational usefulness – although it certainly ticked that box as well. Constructed in Glasgow for the LSWR in 1885, the loco had a varied history, having been sold to the East Kent Railway in 1919 before being acquired by the Southern Railway in 1946 to join the other two surviving members of the class on the Lyme Regis branch. With all three locomotives being withdrawn by BR in 1961, No 488 was elected to be saved by the Bluebell as the last survivor of the historic and long-lived class. Arriving at Sheffield Park in July 1961, No 488 was pressed into service within a few days and

operated for the rest of the season before being restored to full LSWR livery over the winter period. Less than 12 months after opening, the Bluebell Railway's locomotive fleet had doubled from two to four engines and now included examples of locomotives from all three of the major pre-Grouping constituents of the Southern Railway.

Horsted Keynes

More than 92,000 passengers travelled on the Bluebell Railway during 1961, and the year climaxed with the arrival on the last day of the operating season, 29 October, of the first Bluebell train to enter Horsted Keynes station. (Previously all northbound trains had been terminating at Bluebell Halt on the other side of the road from the BR station.) This was the 1.48pm departure from Sheffield Park, worked by all four Bluebell locomotives – *Stepney* and the Adams 'Radial' at the front and the two 'P' Classes at the rear. For the time being the station, which was still served by the Ardingly branch, remained the property of BR, meaning that a BR pilotman was required to be employed at the Bluebell's expense on every train. Bluebell trains were only allowed access to a single platform at the largely deserted station, and no run-round facilities were provided, meaning that locomotives were still required to top-and-tail every train. Nonetheless the Bluebell now had access to 'proper' stations at each end of its running line and full passenger interchange was now possible with BR. It was a taste of things to come, and when the 1962 season commenced and all trains would run through to Horsted Keynes.

ABOVE Privately preserved GNR 'J52' Class 0-6-0ST No 1247 (right) stands at Sheffield Park on 1 April 1962, while alongside it 'P' Class No 323 *Bluebell* shunts the 'Chesham' set. No 1247 had just arrived at the head of the 'Blue Belle' special from London Bridge, carrying none other than Dr Richard Beeching himself! *S. C. Nash, Bluebell Railway Museum Archive*

RIGHT Holywell (Waterworks) Halt – the station opened by Dr Beeching – is seen looking north in May 1962. *Bluebell Railway Museum Archive*

The day Dr Beeching came to call

The 1962 season began with a somewhat surprising visitor in the form of Dr Richard Beeching. He arrived on 1 April on the 'Blue Belle' railtour, which ran from London Bridge to Sheffield Park, via Haywards Heath, behind privately preserved Great Northern Railway 0-6-0ST No 1247, and ironically on this occasion he was called upon to open a new station. The station in question was Holywell (Waterworks) Halt, which the Bluebell believed could be a valuable source of revenue, being located on an existing bus route. Sadly the station failed to attract many new passengers, and those that did use it mainly came by car, to the disapproval of the local authorities. By the end of the 1962 season only around 50 tickets had been sold at Holywell and the station that Beeching had opened quickly closed again after only a few months of use.

The decision to invite Dr Beeching was probably controversial even in 1962, but it was perhaps not as unexpected as it appears. Beeching was a prominent local resident, living as he did in East Grinstead, and was moreover the Chairman of the British Railways Board, an organisation with which the Bluebell would have been keen to maintain a good relationship. The BRB was the Bluebell's landlord at this stage, and it was also from the BRB that the Bluebell was purchasing most of its rolling stock. Beeching of course had had no involvement in the closure of the Bluebell line in the 1950s, and at that time was yet to publish his infamous report. The Bluebell was not the only railway to receive Beeching as an honoured guest in the 1960s (in 1969 he was invited to open the South Devon Railway – then the Dart Valley), and in his defence he was not necessarily anti-rail per se. What Beeching was opposed to was loss-making lines operated under the auspices of the British Railways Board. The existence of a privately run, volunteer-operated railway like the Bluebell would not have troubled him, whether it made a profit or not.

ABOVE Ex-North London Railway tank engine No 2650 is pictured at Sheffield Park circa 1962. *Kevin Robertson*

ABOVE RIGHT Ex-GWR 'Dukedog' Class No 3217 *Earl of Berkeley*, seen here attacking Freshfield Bank in 1967, was the first tender engine to run on the preserved Bluebell Railway when it arrived on the line in February 1962. *Mike Esau, Bluebell Railway Museum Archive*

RIGHT 'E4' Class No. 473 (*Birch Grove*) poses at Horsted Keynes. The loco's lined black livery suggests that this was taken within a few months of its arrival on the Bluebell in October 1962. *Kevin Robertson*

Further arrivals

Prior to Beeching's visit two further locomotives had arrived at the Bluebell in early 1962, each the last survivor of its type. March 1962 had witnessed the arrival of ex-North London Railway tank engine No 2650, dating from 1880 and built primarily for shunting in London's docks, while privately preserved ex-GWR 'Dukedog' No 9017 had arrived in February. The latter, the last surviving locomotive in British Railways service with outside frames, was notable for a number of reasons. Being the first tender engine to operate on the preserved Bluebell line, the 'Dukedog' was considerably larger than any of the other locomotives then present at Sheffield Park and, like the NLR tank, did not hail from a constituent company of the Southern Railway – indeed, to this day it is the only Great Western loco to be based on the Bluebell. Nonetheless, its arrival did allow the railway to claim (not entirely accurately) that its locomotive collection represented 'all the railways in the South of England over the last 90 years'[47]. Interestingly, efforts to preserve No 9017 on the Bluebell had been ongoing since the line's first year of operation when a Mr T. R. Gomm of Birmingham had written to *The Railway Magazine* with the following appeal:

'Sir, I am opening a preservation fund with the object of saving 4-4-0 locomotive No 9017 from the scrap heap… The Western Region is unable to preserve one of this type, but is offering No 9017 for sale for £1,500. If this sum can be raised, the locomotive will go to the Bluebell Line, where it will be used from time to time, mechanical condition permitting, and will be on public exhibition…'[48]

Nominally introduced in 1936, the 'Dukedogs' were in reality a rebuild of two late-Victorian classes, the 'Duke' Class dating from 1895 and the 'Bulldog' Class of 1898, and as such No 9017 would have fitted in well with the Victorian/Edwardian era then evoked by much of the Bluebell's rolling stock. In preservation, No 9017 was quickly adorned with *Earl of Berkeley* nameplates, a name allocated by the GWR in the 1930s but never actually carried in service. Initially retaining BR black livery, it was to remain in this form until 1965, when it received full GWR livery together with its original number of 3217.

Towards the end of the 1962 operating season, on 16 October, a third new locomotive arrived in the form of 'E4' Class 0-6-0T No 32473. As an ex-LBSCR engine, No 32473, swiftly renumbered to its original identity as 473, would have been particularly welcomed by many Bluebell members at the time and was quickly pressed into service on 21 October, the occasion of the 'Victory Belle' railtour from Victoria to Sheffield Park. The tour in question was steam-hauled from London to Haywards Heath by preserved 'T9' 4-4-0 No 120, after which Bluebell traction took over, *Stepney* and the Adams 'Radial' tank working over the Ardingly branch and the newly arrived 'E4' taking over for the final section from Horsted Keynes to Sheffield Park. The 'Victory Belle' was the second railtour of 1962 to run through from BR metals to Sheffield Park, a route that would not be possible for much longer.

The winter of 1962/63 would see both No 473 and 'P' Class No 27 restored to their pre-Grouping liveries, the former reacquiring its original name *Birch Grove* and the latter losing its modern name *Primrose*.

Mixed fortunes

1963 would prove a year of mixed fortunes for the Bluebell Railway. The unsuccessful Holywell Halt was now closed (it would be demolished the following winter). The ex-LNWR observation coach that was to form a mainstay of the Bluebell's passenger fleet arrived in February but no new locomotives entered into stock throughout the year. Opportunities to save rare and important locomotives and rolling stock were having to be passed over as the railway struggled to clear its debts, pay its annual lease and (with the lease due to expire in 1965) save up funds to purchase the trackbed outright. More successful railtours ran through from BR over the Ardingly branch, but by the end of the year the branch would be closed and the Bluebell would be isolated from the national network. In the meantime the publication of the 'Beeching Report' in March 1963 (12 months after Beeching had been an honoured guest at the Bluebell) would herald the closure of hundreds of other lines across Britain.

Railtours

The first railtour to visit the Bluebell in 1963 was the 'Spring Belle', which ran from Victoria to Sheffield Park on 31 March. The Bluebell's own No 473 *Birch Grove* was granted permission

to run on the main line and assisted BR Standard 4MT No 80084 on the southbound run from London to Haywards Heath, from which point the Adams 'Radial' joined *Birch Grove* over the Ardingly branch and on to the Bluebell. Later that year would see the operation of what proved to be the final through train from London to Sheffield Park for several decades. The 'Scottish Belle' on 15 September 1963 also ran from Victoria, on this occasion hauled by restored Caledonian Railway 'Single' No 123 and LSWR Class 'T9' No 120 as far as Haywards Heath, from where *Birch Grove* and the 'Radial' once again took over for the run over the Ardingly branch. (On both occasions the need for engines to be removed at Haywards Heath was so that they could be turned at Brighton for the return trip to London.) Little over a month later the Ardingly branch would close, but the final day would see one final steam-hauled swansong.

Closure of the Ardingly branch

If Bluebell members had hoped that the advantages of direct interchange between BR and Bluebell trains at Horsted Keynes might have been enough to revive the ailing fortunes of the Ardingly branch, they were disappointed when closure of the latter was announced for 28 October 1963. For the final day, the 27th, a steam railtour was arranged, with both *Stepney* and *Birch Grove* allowed out onto the main line to haul the 'Brighton Blue Belle' from Brighton to Sheffield Park and back. On arrival at Horsted Keynes, *Bluebell* took the train forwards to Sheffield Park while *Stepney* and *Birch Grove* remained on the rear. The final electric working over the branch, in the form of 6-PAN unit No 3033, departed from Horsted Keynes at 6.16pm, while the very last passenger service was the return working of the 'Brighton Blue Belle', which pulled out of

ABOVE 'Alight here for the Bluebell Line' proclaims the running-in board at Horsted Keynes as 2-HAL unit No 2651 prepares to depart with a Seaford service in August 1963. Two months later the Ardingly branch would close and the station would cease to be an interchange.
Bluebell Railway Museum Archive

Horsted Keynes at 6.25pm, once again behind *Stepney* and *Birch Grove*. The 27th would not quite be the final occasion on which Bluebell locomotives ventured out towards Ardingly, but passenger services had now ceased and the line was officially closed. The Bluebell had no funds to purchase the branch, so now found itself without a connection to the national network.

Stepney the Bluebell Engine

One happier development in 1963 was the publication of *Stepney the Bluebell Engine* by the Rev W. Awdry. The 18th title in Awdry's 'Railway Series' tells the story of *Stepney*'s visit to the Island of Sodor to meet with Thomas the Tank Engine and friends, and proved a welcome bit of publicity for the Bluebell Railway. (A number of other Bluebell locomotives also make non-speaking cameos in the book, but without the famous 'Thomas' faces.) The global success of the 'Thomas' brand in the decades that followed mean that *Stepney* has become one of the most well-recognised locomotives in British railway preservation.

Tracklifting

The final train over the Ardingly branch, before the demolition contractors took possession, was another Bluebell working. In 1960 the fledgling BRPS had been frustrated in its desire to acquire a second Stroudley 'Terrier' after *Stepney*, and had settled instead for 'P' Class No 323, which was swiftly christened *Bluebell*. However, the closure of the Hayling Island branch in November 1963 meant that more 'Terriers' became available, and in 1964 the Bluebell achieved its aim of owning

ABOVE Ex-LBSCR 'A1X' Class 'Terrier' No 32636 is seen at Sheffield Park still in full BR livery on 20 May 1964, only a few days after its arrival on the Bluebell. Leslie Matthey, then Chairman of the BRPS, is at the controls. Delivered under its own steam on 14 May, No 32636 (better known as No 672 *Fenchurch*) was the very last locomotive to traverse the Ardingly branch before tracklifting began.

K. D. Chown, Bluebell Railway Museum Archive

ABOVE Bluebell steam returned to the closed Ardingly branch when the demolition contractors' own diesel shunter failed on its first day and Bluebell locomotives were instead hired in to cover the work. North London tank No 2650, the regular engine employed on these trains, is seen here pushing eight trucks across Sheriff Mill Viaduct towards Ardingly on 19 September 1964. *Tom Martin, Bluebell Railway Museum Archive*

a second example with the purchase of No 32636, at that time reputed to be the oldest working standard-gauge locomotive in the country. On 14 May 1964 No 32636 traversed the Ardingly branch under its own steam, accompanied by ex-LBSCR milk van No 270, also recently acquired by the Bluebell, becoming in the process the final working on the branch while still under BR ownership, and the last of many Bluebell acquisitions to arrive by rail via Haywards Heath.

Tracklifting on the route throughout between Ardingly and East Grinstead commenced on 15 July 1964. (The short section between Haywards Heath and Ardingly was to be retained to serve the stone terminal located at the latter location.) The demolition contractors set up their base at Ardingly with the intention of working northwards, and the failure of their own Ruston & Hornsby diesel shunter on the first day quickly necessitated the hire of a suitable locomotive from the nearest convenient source – the Bluebell Railway. Thus it was that steam once again returned to the Ardingly branch, and the Bluebell found itself in the unlikely position of actively assisting in the demolition of the routes to both Ardingly and East Grinstead (earning itself some much-needed extra income in the process). The ex-North London Railway tank engine became the contractor's regular engine, crewed by Bluebell enginemen, with No 473 *Birch Grove* deputising when No 2650 was required to return to Sheffield Park for boiler washouts and maintenance. No 473 must have been a familiar site on the branch by this time, having appeared twice on railtours in the previous year.

By late September tracklifting had reached as far as Horsted Keynes, and the 30th saw all physical connection between the Bluebell Railway and the BR network severed. On the positive side, this meant that Bluebell staff were able to take over operation of the now redundant Horsted Keynes signal box (by this time the Bluebell was already renting the station for £400 per annum). Resignalling of Horsted Keynes meant that for the 1965 season the Bluebell would finally have run-round facilities there, allowing an end to the practice of top-and-tailing trains, which had been in place since the line reopened in 1960.

With the rail connection severed, the NLR tank engine was now isolated on the northern section of the line, being temporarily based first at West Hoathly, then Kingscote, as the contractors moved northwards. Lifting of the track was finally completed in March 1965, and on 2 April the engine returned by road from East Grinstead to Sheffield Park. Few at the time could have imagined that it would one day be possible for the locomotive to return to East Grinstead by rail.

An uncertain future?

By the mid-1960s the Bluebell Railway appeared to be increasingly successful; the company had cleared its bank overdraft by 1963/64, a sizeable collection of largely pre-Grouping locomotives and rolling stock had been assembled at Sheffield Park, and passenger numbers continued to increase, with 200,000 being carried during the 1965 season. Yet for all its success, the railway faced an uncertain future. Both its stations, Sheffield Park and Horsted Keynes, and all of the trackbed in between continued to be hired from the British Railways Board under the terms of the lease taken out in 1960 – a lease that was due to expire in 1965.

By this time it was clear neither the Bluebell nor British Railways was keen on allowing the lease to continue indefinitely. BR for its part was no longer interested in leasing unwanted property, preferring to sell it outright, while for the Bluebell it was clear that the lease was a continuing drain upon its limited financial resources. Indeed, the lease agreement had only ever been a last-resort option for the Bluebell, entered into when it became clear that the society was unable to raise enough funds to purchase the line for the sum BR was asking in 1959.

Negotiations

Negotiations with a view to purchasing the line outright when the lease expired were entered into in 1964 and did not get off to a promising start when it was discovered that BR was now asking £65,000 for the line. This was far in excess of anything the Bluebell possessed or could hope to raise from its members – and almost double the sum of £34,000 for which BR had offered to sell the same section of track in 1959! Nonetheless, negotiations between the two parties continued. The lease, which technically expired in 1965, now began to be extended yearly on a piecemeal basis while the Bluebell set up a 'Line Purchase Scheme' with the aim of raising at least £20,000 towards the eventual cost of purchasing the line. Things were clearly looking serious, as the 1966 Guidebook pleaded: 'The future success or failure of the Bluebell Railway depends entirely on the success of this scheme… Please help all you can.'[49]

BELOW By the end of March 1965 lifting of the track from Ardingly to East Grinstead was complete and NLR tank No 2650, on hire to the demolition contractors, was marooned at the northern end of the line. Pictured here at East Grinstead on 20 March 1965, with the main-line station in the background, No 2650 is standing very approximately where the Bluebell Railway station stands today. *S. C. Nash, Bluebell Railway Museum Archive*

One factor that the Bluebell did have in its favour at this time was that, realistically, there were no other obvious buyers for the Sheffield Park to Horsted Keynes trackbed. Doubtless the route could have been divided up into individual parcels of land and sold to those landowners whose property abutted onto the railway, as had already been done with the rest of the Lewes to East Grinstead line. However, in order to do so BR would first have to arrange for the route to be stripped of all existing railway infrastructure, such as track, signalling, etc. This in itself would be no easy task now that the preserved section was completely isolated, by several miles in each direction, from the rest of the national network – all contractor's equipment would have to arrive by road and all redundant trackwork, etc, would have to be removed in the same way. Moreover, the Bluebell Railway by now was successful, popular and famous, even internationally famous. To force its premature closure would arguably be a publicity disaster for the newly re-branded British Rail. Clearly the most profitable and practical option would be to agree a price and sell the entire Sheffield Park to Horsted Keynes route to the one group of people who actually wanted to purchase it with all track and equipment in situ – the Bluebell Railway itself.

Purchase

In late 1967, by which time the Bluebell had succeeded in raising £22,000, a purchase price of £43,500 was agreed for the route, including the stations and surrounding land at both Sheffield Park and Horsted Keynes. Initially BR was still demanding the total amount up front but, when the Bluebell proved unable to raise a bank loan for the balance, a further agreement was reached in the spring of 1968 whereby BR would accept a down payment of £23,500, with the balance of £20,000 to be paid in instalments over the following five years. On 27 October 1968 contracts were exchanged and the Bluebell took formal possession of the Sheffield Park to Horsted Keynes railway line. After eight years of operation, the Bluebell Railway finally 'owned' its own line.

The end of decade

By the end of the 1960s the landscape of Britain's railways had changed forever. When the newly formed Bluebell Railway had operated its first passenger service in 1960 steam had still been the predominant motive power across most of the national network. Only a decade later diesel and electric traction reigned supreme, with steam having been completely eliminated from all BR lines by the end of 1968. Thousands of steam locomotives had been sold for scrap, some of them less than a decade after being built. The 'Beeching axe' had fallen on many lines as well, with thousands of route miles having closed since 1963, following on from the closure programmes that had seen the former LEGR axed in the 1950s. The railway world of 1970 was considerably leaner than that into which the Bluebell Railway had emerged in 1960.

The world of heritage railways was also changing by the end of the decade. In 1960 the Bluebell Railway had been the only standard-gauge preserved passenger line in the UK. Ten years later others, such as the Keighley & Worth Valley Railway in 1968 and the original Dart Valley Railway (now the South Devon Railway) in 1969, were starting to follow where the Bluebell pioneers had led. Many more would spring up over the next few years. Perversely, the cuts and closures of the 1960s had proved something of a boon to the preservation

ABOVE On 27 October 1968 the Bluebell Railway exchanged contracts with British Rail and formally took possession of the Sheffield Park-Horsted Keynes trackbed. On the same day the occasion was celebrated by a commemorative 'Blue Belle' special double-headed by ex-SECR 'P' Class Nos 27 and 323 *Bluebell*. *K. D. Chown, Bluebell Railway Museum Archive*

ABOVE 'Terrier' No 72 *Fenchurch* shelters in the Bluebell Railway's original engine shed on 2 July 1968. Constructed in 1960, this was virtually the only covered accommodation the Bluebell's rolling stock had in its first decade. Although superseded by many larger structures, the shed would remain standing at Sheffield Park until storm damage led to its demolition in January 2014. *Len Walton*

movement, providing not only the impetus for enthusiasts to preserve the steam railway before it was lost forever, but also creating a ready supply of recently disused lines and unwanted locomotives that could be taken on by those who could raise the funds to do so.

Bluebell changes

The Bluebell Railway had also changed over the course of the decade. When it had opened in August 1960 it had owned the grand total of two coaches and two locomotives, and had operated at weekends only for three months before closing for the winter. By 1968 the railway had a sizeable fleet of locomotives and coaching stock and operated passenger services for 197 days of the year, with a two-train service being successfully piloted on summer Sunday afternoons.

By 1970 the Bluebell had also begun to employ larger locomotives and more modern rolling stock, moving away from its original aim of evoking solely a sleepy railway backwater in the pre-Grouping era. This gradual change in policy was largely practical. The railway's growing popularity meant that longer, heavier trains were required to carry the ever-increasing numbers of visitors – trains that were increasingly beyond the capacity of the six-wheeled tank engines that had originally provided the mainstay of the line's fleet. For some years the 1938-built GWR 'Dukedog' loco had been both the largest and youngest engine (and, indeed, the only tender engine) based on the Bluebell, but that position was to change dramatically in 1969 with the arrival of ex-BR Standard Class 4MT No 75027. Purchased on the Bluebell's behalf by a private donor, No 75027 was the first tender loco to be owned outright by the Bluebell

ABOVE 'P' Class No 27, formerly *Primrose* but by now restored to full SECR livery, waits to return from Horsted Keynes to Sheffield Park with the ex-LNWR observation coach on a damp 11 January 1969. *Len Walton*

BELOW BR Standard Class 4MT No 75027 arrives at the Bluebell in January 1969. Paid for anonymously by the late Charlie Pyne, a BRPS member, the arrival of No 75027 signalled a major change of direction for a railway that had once seemingly specialised in the preservation of small pre-Grouping tank engines. *K. D. Chown, Bluebell Railway Museum Archive*

ABOVE The problems of storing historic wooden-bodied carriages in the open air in all weathers are amply demonstrated in this view of Horsted Keynes on 29 November 1969. 'Terrier' No 72 *Fenchurch* waits to depart for Sheffield Park. *Len Walton*

ABOVE 'P' Class No 323 *Bluebell* displays its 'Bluebell blue' livery, first applied in 1966, as it takes water at Sheffield Park after working a train from Horsted Keynes on 26 October 1969. *Len Walton*

BELOW On 7 August 1970 the Bluebell Railway celebrated its first ten years of operation. Ex-LBSCR Class 'E4' No 473 *Birch Grove*, double-heading with 'Dukedog' No 3217 *Earl of Berkeley*, is seen here carrying 'The Decadian' headboard at Horsted Keynes. *Ken Grinstead, Bluebell Railway Museum Archive*

ABOVE The lack of overhaul facilities at Sheffield Park led to ex-LSWR Adams 'Radial' tank No 488 being dispatched to Swindon Works for repair in October 1971. Seen here inside the works on 27 October, the driving wheels have already been removed and the locomotive stands in front of Western Region diesel-hydraulic No D1011 *Western Thunderer*. Ironically the modern diesel locomotive would be withdrawn for scrapping only four years later, while the Victorian steam engine had its long-term future assured. *R. C. H. Nash, Bluebell Railway Museum Archive*

(the 'Dukedog' being privately preserved), and was the first BR-built loco to run over the route since the Lewes to East Grinstead line had closed in 1958. Indeed, having been built as recently as 1954, No 75027 was only six years older than the preserved line itself! Arguably its acquisition reflected not only the Bluebell's need for more powerful locomotives but also the rapid changes that had swept over Britain's railways during the 1960s. What would have passed for a modern, almost new, locomotive in 1960 was by 1969 a historic relic of a previous era, worthy only of scrapping or preservation.

Meanwhile a chronic lack of covered accommodation for rolling stock was taking its toll; many of the wooden-bodied carriages that had provided the Bluebell's original fleet were by now suffering badly from constant exposure to the elements and were having to be taken out of service. 1970 was to see the first entry into service of two Bulleid-designed Southern Railway carriages, while the historic 'Chesham set' was by now entirely out of service (the full four-car set would not see operational use again until the 21st century). Many more coaches of Bulleid, and BR, design were to follow over the coming decades. With the urgent need to raise funds for the purchase of the line now in the past, the Bluebell was finally in a position to start

addressing this lack of covered accommodation, and 1970 would also see the launch of an appeal to raise £7,000 for the construction of a four-road carriage shed.

Thus it was that by the start of the 1970s the Bluebell Railway had survived its first decade to become a successful and secure heritage attraction, it had successfully purchased its own line from BR, and had survived unscathed the loss of its connection to the national network when the Ardingly branch closed. Its long-term future was secure and it seemed content to continue as an isolated 4½-line in rural Sussex. The following decade would see the first signs that the Bluebell still had ambitious plans for the future.

CHAPTER NINE

·····················

The northern extension

The title clause of the Bluebell Railway Company,
as set out in February 1960, includes the following commitment:

'To purchase, take upon lease or otherwise acquire all or any interest in the
railway now existing between East Grinstead and Lewes in the County of Sussex
or any part thereof and all land, buildings or equipment, rolling stock, effects
and other property…'[50]

Despite these lofty aims, throughout its first decade it must have seemed unlikely that the often cash-starved Bluebell Railway would ever acquire any more of the old LEGR than the existing 4½-mile stretch between Horsted Keynes and Sheffield Park. As the 1970s unfolded, however, the Bluebell turned its eyes northwards, first with a modest proposal to extend over a short distance, before ultimately committing itself to a decades-long project that would prove to be one of the most ambitious in the history of British railway preservation.

A northern extension?

The prospect of extending the Bluebell's running line north of Horsted Keynes first appeared in 1972 when the then owner of Horsted House Farm agreed to the possible sale of the five-eighths-of-a-mile trackbed that extended across his property. With negotiations under way, the Bluebell applied successfully for planning permission and launched its first Northern Extension Appeal. Sadly these plans fell through when the farmer in question decided instead to sell the entire farm as a going concern, and the new owner proved unwilling to sell the trackbed.

This failure to extend by even such a short distance could easily have brought an end to the matter, but the notion of extending northward had evidently taken root. Rather than being disheartened, the railway now took the somewhat surprising decision that it should start planning to reconstruct the entire 6 miles of abandoned trackbed north of Horsted Keynes – with the ultimate aim of reconnecting with the national network at East Grinstead. This would be no small achievement considering that the trackbed had been divided into multiple parcels of land and was now in the hands of around 30 different owners – and the Bluebell had just failed in its first attempt to buy even five-eighths of a mile from one of them.

West Hoathly

In 1975 the Bluebell took its first serious step towards extending when the opportunity arose to purchase the site of West Hoathly station. More than 2 miles to the north of Horsted Keynes, the station itself had been demolished in 1967 and the whole site cleared for housing development. Although

ABOVE Demolition is under way at West Hoathly on 14 November 1964. The contractors' Ruston & Hornsby diesel shunter (the failure of which led to the hire of Bluebell steam engines to carry out the work) can be seen parked behind the rubble strewn across the down line.
E. Wilmshurst, Bluebell Railway Museum Archive

planning permission had been granted, development had not taken place and the site was still undeveloped when the Bluebell was made aware of the possibility of buying it in 1975. This would be key to the success of any possible future extension because, if development was allowed to proceed, the route to East Grinstead would be blocked forever – a fate that had already befallen the line south towards Lewes. Appeals for funds were urgently made to Bluebell members and in the autumn of 1975 the site was successfully purchased for £25,000.

It should not be underestimated what a leap of faith this was for the Bluebell at the time. The railway still did not then own any of the trackbed between West Hoathly and Horsted Keynes, West Hoathly station itself had been demolished, and the railway had no planning permission to construct a new station there, or indeed to construct or operate any railway between the two locations. In effect, the Bluebell had simply bought a small plot of land in a location isolated by more than 2 miles from its own operations. Nonetheless, the purchase of West Hoathly had protected the route to East Grinstead from the threat of development and demonstrated that the Bluebell was serious about extending north.

The project described in 1976

Describing the Bluebell's ambitious plans in early 1976, *The Railway Magazine* noted that the trackbed was largely still intact, save for the demolition of one overbridge – New

LEFT An image that symbolises the changing face of the Bluebell Railway at the start of the 1970s. SECR 'P' Class No 27 (built in 1910) double-heads on Freshfield Bank with BR Standard Class 4MT No 75027 (built in 1954) on 19 September 1971. The 0-6-0T 'P' Class loco (formerly known as *Primrose*) typifies the kind of small pre-Grouping loco favoured by the Bluebell in its early years, while the BR 4-6-0, at that time by far the youngest and largest operational loco on the line, demonstrated how far the railway's scope and ambition had developed over its first decade. *Bluebell Railway Museum Archive*

ABOVE The down platform canopy at Kingscote is being demolished in 1976. When the Bluebell accepted the offer to remove the unwanted canopy from the then privately owned station, few of those involved can have imagined that the railway would one day have the opportunity to come back and rebuild it. *Mike Esau, Bluebell Railway Museum Archive*

LEFT One of the events that marked the Bluebell's transition towards larger engines in the 1970s was the arrival in 1971 of the Bulleid Society's 'West Country' Class No 21C123. Following a successful boiler inspection, *Blackmore Vale* became the first 'Pacific' to run on the Bluebell in the preservation era when – minus her 'air-smoothed' casing – she made her maiden test run from Sheffield Park to Horsted Keynes on 2 November 1975. *Mike Esau, Bluebell Railway Museum Archive*

ABOVE With restoration complete, *Blackmore Vale* returned to passenger service in 1976. She is seen here double-heading with 'C' Class No 592 shortly after departing from Sheffield Park with the 4.55pm train for Horsted Keynes on 16 May 1976. *Len Walton*

Coombe Bridge, to the north of West Hoathly. The two largest engineering structures on the line, Sharpthorne Tunnel and Imberhorne Viaduct, were still in the ownership of British Rail – the tunnel being 'maintained to little short of mainline standards', while the viaduct still carried tracks used for carriage stabling south of East Grinstead. Physically the largest obstacle to reopening through to East Grinstead would be the cutting to the south of Imberhorne Viaduct, which at the time was still in use as a municipal rubbish dump, tipping having commenced there in 1968. Amazingly, what would ultimately prove to be one of the most challenging projects ever undertaken by a heritage railway, the clearance of Imberhorne cutting, was described at the time as presenting 'no particular difficulties'!

On the eve of the purchase of the West Hoathly site, *The Railway Magazine* looked optimistically to the future:

'Many months – possibly years – of negotiations with both local landowners and local authorities lie ahead. Once the land is acquired the long-neglected trackbed has to be cleared and drained, track re-laid, signalling installed and new buildings constructed. Many details remain to be settled but at present it is envisaged that by re-opening in stages East Grinstead could be reached in ten to fifteen years time. A formidable task indeed, but one in which Bluebell is determined to succeed.'[51]

Planning permission

If the railway was ever to run trains again to West Hoathly, let alone East Grinstead, planning consent would be required from the local authorities. With planning permission for the trackbed across Horsted House Farm still extant, in January 1976 an application was made to Mid Sussex District Council for the section from Horsted House Farm to the West Hoathly site – only to be rejected by three votes to two. Not to be put off, in 1978 the Bluebell applied again, this time seeking planning permission to reconstruct the line over the entire route from Horsted Keynes to East Grinstead (the earlier permission for the Horsted House Farm section had expired by this point). At this stage, with Kingscote currently a private residence, the proposal was for a single-track line throughout with no intermediate stations. The application faced some powerful opposition, including the Forestry Commission and the National Farmers Union, whose members were in possession of much of the trackbed, and was turned down in 1979. Still undaunted, the Bluebell now formed an Extension Committee, which met for the first time in 1980, and set about the lengthy process of appealing for a public inquiry into the planning refusal while simultaneously preparing an application for a Light Railway Order.

Public inquiry

Four years after planning permission had been refused in 1979 the public inquiry demanded by the railway finally began on 21 June 1983, an application for a Light Railway Order having been made in January of that year. Over the course of three weeks the inquiry heard evidence from the railway and its supporters, including British Rail, the South East Tourist Board and the East Grinstead Chamber of Commerce. Those in opposition included Mid Sussex District Council, which expressed fears about increased noise and traffic levels as well as the feasibility of the project, and the National Farmers Union, which continued to defend its members who owned and used the trackbed for livestock access and other agricultural purposes.

Having heard the arguments and sifted through the evidence, it was almost two years later, on 2 April 1985, that the Inspecting Officer finally made his report to the Secretary of State for the Environment. The initial news was not good; the Inspector recommended that both the planning appeal and Light Railway Order application be dismissed. Fortunately,

however, the Inspector's own recommendations went largely ignored. The power to award a Light Railway Order lay with the Secretary of State for Transport and this was duly granted – in effect clearing the way for the planning application to be approved. Reported *The Times* a few days later:

> 'The Government has given the privately owned Bluebell Railway in West Sussex right of way to link up with British Rail trains at East Grinstead. British Rail have welcomed the idea.
>
> The link will cost £2m and double the track's length from five miles to ten miles.'[52]

Kingscote

One factor that may have influenced the Government's decision to overrule the Inspector was the Bluebell's continuing negotiations with the various owners of the trackbed. One issue raised by the Inspector, based on the evidence heard at the 1983 Inquiry, was the allegedly slim likelihood of much of the trackbed ever becoming available for purchase. In reality, negotiations with landowners had continued over the intervening two years and prospects were beginning to look more positive, with the railway having already acquired one small, but significant, part of the route – Kingscote station.

Unlike West Hoathly, where only the remains of the platforms survived, at Kingscote the main station house had become a private residence and was largely intact, albeit somewhat dilapidated. When the property came onto the market in 1984 the Bluebell immediately expressed interest and in January 1985 the station was acquired for just over £100,000. The surviving building retained its original canopy and stood on the largely extant up platform, while the 3-acre site also included the trackbed, the site of the demolished

ABOVE Kingscote station is seen in 1984, shortly before purchase by the Bluebell Railway. *Bluebell Railway Museum Archive*

down platform, and the partially filled-in subway. It would take many years to return the semi-derelict station to its former glory, but by the end of January a team of Bluebell volunteers had already begun the long work of restoration.

Negotiations

Almost a decade after purchasing the site of West Hoathly, the Bluebell was now in possession of the sites of both intermediate stations between Horsted Keynes and East Grinstead, but none of the railway in between – around 6 miles in total. Fortunately relationships with at least some landowners were now beginning to thaw. Significantly, Horsted House Farm, immediately north of Horsted Keynes, was again under new ownership and the short section of line that had so narrowly slipped through the Bluebell's fingers in 1972 finally looked within reach. Other landowners too were beginning to take a more positive attitude towards the railway, some perhaps more willing to take seriously a concern that now had official sanction, in the form of both planning permission and a Light Railway Order, to reconstruct the Horsted Keynes to East Grinstead line. Certainly the Bluebell had demonstrated that it was in it for the long term and had the determination to see the project through. Compulsory purchase orders were also a theoretical possibility now that the extension had Government authorisation and, while these never became necessary in practice, may well have concentrated the minds of some landowners.

Share issue

With a railway line now to be purchased and reconstructed, not to mention the small matter of a municipal rubbish dump to be excavated at Imberhorne, the Bluebell decided to take a new approach to fundraising. On the 25 November 1985 *The Guardian* announced:

ABOVE **Viewed from the north, the ceremonial laying of the first track panel on the northern extension took place at Leamland Bridge on 13 March 1988. The long march to East Grinstead had begun!** *Mike Esau, Bluebell Railway Museum Archive*

'Members of the steam railway's preservation society yesterday decided to form a public company to raise £2 million to lay six miles of track from the line's present terminus at Horsted Keynes to connect up with British Rail's network at East Grinstead.'[53]

The prospectus for the first share issue, which went on to raise more than £460,000, was issued in early 1986 and provided a summary of the extension project at that time:

'Bluebell seeks to purchase freehold title to plots of the track bed between Horsted Keynes and East Grinstead. At the present time Bluebell owns, can acquire or has commenced negotiations for up to 68% of this trackbed and the intention is to purchase the remainder by negotiation with the existing owners. There is no guarantee that this land will become available.'[54]

The extension begins

In the autumn of 1987, 15 years after negotiations had first taken place with the then owners of Horsted House Farm, the Bluebell Railway finally purchased the trackbed to the immediate north of Horsted Keynes. The long work of reconstructing the route north could finally begin.

The first track panel of the northern extension was laid with much ceremony at Leamland Bridge, for so long the northern limit of the Bluebell's property, on 13 March 1988. Guests of honour, including publisher Ian Allan and Network SouthEast Director Chris Green, were carried to the site behind the North London Railway tank engine, appropriately the very same locomotive that had played a large part in the demolition of the line in the early 1960s. Once there, the Secretary of State for Transport, the Rt Hon Paul Channon MP, was formally invited to operate the Bluebell's own steam crane as the first panel was gently lowered into place. Reported *The Times* the next day:

'Only 50 yards are being laid now as a token start to comply with a Department of the Environment condition that work should begin within seven years of planning approval for the extension being granted in 1985. Yesterday's ceremony was timed to coincide with the thirtieth anniversary of the closure of British Rail's East Grinstead to Lewes line.'[55]

Tracklaying on the short section to Horsted House Bridge now commenced in earnest, and by spring 1990 the Bluebell was ready to mark its 30th anniversary year with the launch of an 'extension shuttle' service to the railway's new northern boundary. The shuttle was to be operated separately from the

main Sheffield Park to Horsted Keynes line, in accordance with a Department of Transport stipulation, and, owing to the lack of run-round facilities at Horsted House Farm Bridge, trains were to be propelled to the buffer stop before being hauled back to Horsted Keynes. Two carriages were selected for the operation, SR Open 3rd No 1309 and SR Maunsell BCK No 6575, the latter being modified so that it could lead the train when being propelled northwards. No station was provided at the northern extremity and the complete round trip, for which passengers were charged an add-on fare, took around 10 minutes. Following a successful Department of Transport inspection of the new line on 1 April, passenger shuttles began operating on 14 April. It was only a short distance, but for the first time in more than three decades it was possible for passengers to catch a northbound train from Horsted Keynes.

Horsted House to West Hoathly

The opening of the extension shuttle was only the start of the railway's ambitions, and in 1991 the push northward continued, funded by the launch of a second share issue. Noted *The Guardian*: 'The money will be used to replace a bridge and to re-lay a further 3½ miles of track.'[56] Within reach now were West Hoathly, the former station site purchased by the railway as long ago as 1975, and beyond that Kingscote.

The 731-yard Sharpthorne Tunnel, immediately south of West Hoathly, had been donated to the Bluebell by British Rail, and by December 1991 track had already been relaid southwards from West Hoathly through the tunnel, where on 29 February 1992 it connected with tracks that had been laid in a northerly direction from Horsted House. On 5 March a train passed through the tunnel for the first time since 1964 and, just over a month later, 'Merchant Navy' Class 'Pacific' No 35027 Port Line hauled the first public train service to arrive at West Hoathly since 1958. Finances and planning restrictions prevented the construction of a new station at West Hoathly, but a run-round loop was installed to the south of the site of

ABOVE LEFT Horsted House Bridge, the Bluebell's new northern boundary, is seen on 27 September 1989. Several months before the launch of the extension shuttle trains, the newly laid track is already in situ. The brick wall still blocking one side of the bridge at this stage was a leftover from the site's previous use as a rifle-range. *Norman Sherry, Bluebell Railway Museum Archive*

ABOVE RIGHT The long-closed north portal of Sharpthorne Tunnel, protected by iron railings, is seen on 3 October 1989. *Norman Sherry, Bluebell Railway Museum Archives*

ABOVE Ballasting work is being undertaken at the northern end of Sharpthorne Tunnel on 8 August 1991. *Mike Esau, Bluebell Railway Museum Archives*

New Coombe Bridge (demolished in the winter of 1964-65), meaning that trains over the northern extension would no longer need to be propelled north from Horsted Keynes. No 35027, which was based on the Bluebell at the time, was on duty again on 16 May when it broke through a banner for the official reopening to West Hoathly.

New Coombe Bridge

Other than the infilled cutting at Imberhorne, the single largest engineering obstacle to the reinstatement of the railway line between Horsted Keynes and East Grinstead was the missing bridge at New Coombe, just north of West Hoathly. Faced with an estimated cost of around £200,000 for the design and construction of a new bridge, the Bluebell was instead fortunate to purchase a second-hand bridge that had been used to carry railborne aggregate loads during the reconstruction of the A55 in North Wales. With the last of three spans successfully lifted onto newly constructed abutments at New Coombe on 10 May 1993, an engineer's train, hauled by LSWR 'B4' Class No 96 *Normandy*, passed onto the bridge at around 5.00pm the same day. For a final cost of around only £43,000 the Bluebell had literally bridged the gap in the next stage of its extension. Next stop Kingscote!

Return to Kingscote

With the station having been acquired by the Bluebell nine years earlier, much had changed at Kingscote by the time tracklaying commenced on the New Coombe to Kingscote section in January 1994. Over the intervening years a team of dedicated volunteers had worked to return the semi-derelict building to its former glory: structural alterations had been reversed; rotten floors renewed; plumbing renewed; missing fireplaces, doors and canopy supports replaced; fences built; and the subway excavated. The demolished down platform, together with the northern part of the up platform and the Gents toilet block, had all been reconstructed. Most impressive, perhaps, was the reinstatement of the long-lost canopy on the down platform. As long ago as 1976 the then owner of Kingscote had offered to donate the down canopy to the Bluebell Railway, on condition that they demolish it and take it away for free. Having bought the site and rebuilt the missing platform, the Bluebell was now able to reconstruct the

TOP LEFT Engineering work continues on the 'new' New Coombe Bridge on 22 May 1993, less than two weeks after the final span was lifted into place. *R. Bamberough, Bluebell Railway Museum Archives*

TOP RIGHT Reconstruction of Platform 2 is well under way but much is still to be done in this circa 1992 shot of Kingscote. Just two years later the station would be ready to receive its first passengers. *Michael Hopps*

ABOVE The wet weather does nothing to dampen spirits as appropriately decorated SECR 'C' Class 0-6-0 No 592 hauls the official reopening train into Kingscote station on 21 May 1994. The first Bluebell passenger service into Kingscote, also pulled by No 592, had actually arrived at Kingscote a month earlier on 23 April. *Bluebell Railway Museum Archives*

canopy using many of the parts that had been removed almost 20 years earlier.

With tracklaying largely complete, 'B4' Class *Normandy* arrived at the station with a works train on 19 March 1994. Exactly one month later the reconstructed line passed a

Department of Transport inspection and on 23 April the first public passenger service to call at Kingscote since 1955 was hauled by SECR 'C' Class No 592. The same loco was again on duty on 21 May 1994 when it was decorated to haul the official reopening train.

The formerly sleepy Kingscote now entered perhaps the busiest period in its entire career as it became the northern terminus of the extended Bluebell Railway for almost a decade. With planning restrictions preventing the construction of a car park, a bus link was introduced to bridge the 2-mile gap between Kingscote and East Grinstead. The northern extension project, having come so far, was now about to face its greatest engineering challenge.

Imberhorne Viaduct and East Grinstead station

While work had been under way to extend towards Kingscote, efforts had also been made to secure the northern end of the route, specifically the imposing Imberhorne Viaduct (also known as Hill Place Viaduct) and interchange facilities at East Grinstead station itself.

The ten-arch Imberhorne Viaduct, which had remained in British Rail ownership since the closure of the line, was formally handed over to the Bluebell at a ceremony conducted on the viaduct on 8 September 1992. On the day a special train was hauled from London Bridge to the viaduct by Class 73 No

ABOVE The buffer stops at the south end of Imberhorne Viaduct are seen here in April 1990. For many years these overgrown sidings marked the absolute southern boundary of British Rail's route from London to East Grinstead. *Norman Sherry, Bluebell Railway Museum Archives*

ABOVE This undated 1990s view shows a Network SouthEast departure board at East Grinstead advising passengers to 'Change here for Bluebell Railway Services to Kingscote, West Hoathly, Horsted Keynes and Sheffield Park'. What it doesn't mention is that the first part of the journey, to Kingscote, will be by bus! (Also, the inclusion of West Hoathly is odd as Bluebell Railway trains have never stopped there.) *Bluebell Railway Museum Archive*

73133 *The Bluebell Railway* (the second member of its class to carry this name), and the Bluebell accepted ownership of the 262-yard-long structure in return for a nominal fee of only £1.00. This was a win-win situation for both parties, as the Bluebell was taking over from BR responsibility for the maintenance of the Grade II listed viaduct, with initial repairs to the arches and parapets soon coming to £175,000. For its part, the Bluebell was gaining ownership of the immediate southern approach to East Grinstead station and further cementing its claim to the land on which to build an interchange station in the town itself. Or so it was thought…

In fact, the proposed site for the Bluebell's East Grinstead station, immediately to the south of the existing BR station, had been effectively agreed as far back as the 1980s, an agreement that was further bolstered by the handover of Imberhorne Viaduct in 1992. Unfortunately the Bluebell's agreement was with BR, and by the mid-1990s BR was being wound up and its property handed over to Railtrack. In October 1995 a planning application was launched by Sainsbury's, which already had a supermarket adjacent to the station, to resite its car park on land previously reserved for the Bluebell's new station. Naturally the Bluebell launched a planning appeal, but it would take several years of negotiations between Sainsbury's, the Bluebell and Railtrack – and then Network Rail when the land changed ownership again – before a suitable compromise was reached between all parties.

By the late 1990s enough time had passed for the rubbish to have stabilised, and in 1997 permission was granted to sink a number of trial pits into the tip to test the contents and the rate of decomposition. In this way the railway was able to confirm that the cutting contained no major surprises (among the items excavated were a milk churn, a washing machine and a newspaper from 1969), and other than a small amount of asbestos no hazardous materials were uncovered. The clay capping was found to be around 2.5 metres deep and evidence of the original track ballast was discovered, apparently still in situ, at the bottom of one of the test pits. The way was now clear for the Bluebell to plan the eventual excavation of the cutting.

Imberhorne cutting

As mentioned above, Imberhorne cutting had been acquired by East Grinstead Council in the 1960s and used for dumping domestic waste. Tipping began in 1968 and continued until the mid-1970s, by which time the entire 400-yard cutting had been infilled to the brim with around 130,000 cubic yards of material. Consisting of around 96,000 cubic yards of domestic waste and 34,000 cubic yards of clay capping material, the tip extended from Hill Place Farm Bridge in the north to just south of Imberhorne Lane Bridge. Such was the depth of the material that the parapets of the two bridges, which had once stood high above the railway, now appeared to be at ground level. The Bluebell would have to safely excavate, remove and dispose of at least most of this material if trains were ever to run from Kingscote to East Grinstead again.

RIGHT The first track panel between Kingscote and East Grinstead was laid with due ceremony by the Lady Mayor of East Grinstead, Beverly Heasman, on 29 October 2003. The locomotive used for the occasion was BR Standard Class 4MT 2-6-4T No 80151, representing a type of loco that worked many trains over the route during the final years of BR operation in the 1950s. *Bluebell Railway Museum Archive*

Imberhorne Lane Bridge

Tracks were laid from Kingscote to the southern end of the cutting by the autumn of 2004, and on 6 June 2005 Ivatt Class 2 2-6-2 tank No 41312, on loan to the Bluebell at the time, hauled the first southbound train of excavated spoil from the site. This initial phase of the operation was intended to remove the material that occupied the area to the south of Imberhorne Lane Bridge (which was actually spoil dumped during the construction of Beeching Way). Although relatively low key compared to what was to follow later, this would still amount to around 18,000 cubic metres of material. For the next few years trains hauled by a variety of steam locomotives and

ABOVE Viewed from the parapet of the still partially buried Imberhorne Lane Bridge, the early stages of spoil clearance from the southern end of the cutting are seen on 8 August 2005. *Michael Hopps*

BELOW In early 2009 the Bluebell hired in Class 73 No 73136 *Perseverance* to assist in the regular spoil trains operating from south of Imberhorne Lane Bridge. On 13 March the electro-diesel is seen heading south towards Sharpthorne Tunnel with four loaded wagons. *Keith Duke*

diesel shunters, as well as electro-diesel Class 73 No 73136 *Perseverance*, on loan for two months during 2009, would depart from the site with around three or four wagonloads of spoil. No domestic waste was being removed at this stage and much of the excavated material was recycled to build up the formation of the spur from Horsted Keynes towards the demolished Sheriff Mill Viaduct on the Ardingly branch, which was by now in the hands of the Bluebell. By the autumn of 2005 the southern side of Imberhorne Lane Bridge was already beginning to be exposed, although it would be 2008 before both sides of the bridge had been excavated to trackbed level and tracks laid underneath. By this time moves were well under way to tackle the tip from the northern end as well.

Waste removal

In 2007, having been removing spoil from the south side of Imberhorne Lane Bridge since 2005, the Bluebell Railway finally signed an agreement with West Sussex County Council to purchase and remove the entire tip between the bridges at Imberhorne Lane and Hill Place Farm. Wrote *The Railway Magazine*: 'This deal is crucial, being the final piece of land required to complete the Kingscote to East Grinstead extension.'[57] With the project funded in part by the launch of a third share

ABOVE LEFT Before tracklaying could commence it was necessary for Bluebell volunteers to lay a waterproof membrane across Imberhorne Viaduct, as seen in this image from 18 November 2009. *Michael Hopps*

ABOVE RIGHT With waste clearance finally under way, tracks into the cutting had penetrated a short distance south of Hill Place Farm Bridge by 21 March 2011. *Michael Hopps*

BELOW The scale of the work still to be done is clear in this view of the tip face taken on 11 July 2011. Less than two years later the cutting would be clear and trains would be running through from East Grinstead to Sheffield Park. *Michael Hopps*

issue, on 25 November 2008 a group of invited guests, including the Mayor of East Grinstead, witnessed the first lorry load of waste depart from the site of Hill Place Farm Bridge at the northern end of the cutting. This initial phase would see around 10 metres of cutting being cleared per week, with around 35 lorries leaving the site every day, each carrying almost 20 tons of excavated domestic waste.[58] But soon a more efficient and environmentally sound option would become available.

Connection at East Grinstead

With negotiations over the site of the proposed Bluebell station complete, it became possible for tracklaying to begin southward from East Grinstead, and on 14 January 2009 the

northern end of the Bluebell was reconnected to the national network. At this stage, with Imberhorne cutting still very much blocked, the Bluebell's new northern outpost was isolated from its actual running line. Nonetheless the connection had much more than symbolic value as it would soon enable the removal of waste from Imberhorne by rail. In the meantime the historic connection was ceremonially marked on Saturday 17 January 2009 when Class 73 No 73109 *Battle of Britain – 50th Anniversary* propelled 4-VEP unit No 3417 onto Bluebell metals as far as the viaduct gates. Named after ex-Southern Region General Manager (and future Bluebell President) Gordon Pettitt, the slam-door unit was then transferred to Bluebell ownership by South West Trains, becoming the first Bluebell-owned train ever to depart from East Grinstead.

While work proceeded on construction of a platform at East Grinstead, tracklaying also continued towards the northern face of the tip, and July 2010 saw the first trainload of railborne waste depart northward via East Grinstead. Operated by GBRf, the waste trains were hauled by Class 66 locomotives and consisted of initially 18 MLA wagons (this was ultimately increased to 20 wagons). Each departure carried around 1,000 tons of waste – equivalent to 50 lorries' worth – destined for Forder's Sidings, a

landfill site in Calvert, Buckinghamshire. The next two years would see several phases of 'Waste by Rail' during which loaded trains would depart on a daily basis, moving in total around 70,000 tons of domestic waste to its new home. (Fortunately the entire contents of the tip did not need to be removed as the Bluebell only required to lay a single track line through the formerly double-tracked cutting.) As the cutting was slowly cleared from the northern end, so the ballast and trackwork slowly progressed into the cutting, inching ever closer to the Bluebell's existing running line to the south.

Railtours

Although the cutting remained blocked, the new Bluebell station at East Grinstead formally opened on 4 September 2010. A number of fundraising 'open weekends' now began to take place at which passengers could pay to travel the short distance across Imberhorne Viaduct on the Bluebell's own 4-VEP unit No 3417 *Gordon Pettitt*, usually propelled by a Class 73 electro-

diesel supplied by GBRf. However, the honour of operating the first through railtour onto Bluebell tracks since the loss of the Ardingly branch in 1963 was to fall to preserved 'Hastings' DEMU No 1001 when it operated the 'Hastings Blue Belle' charter from Hastings, via London Bridge and East Grinstead, to the northern face of Imberhorne tip and back on 6 November 2010; indeed, this was the first through passenger service to operate south of East Grinstead since 1960. The following year, on 5 November 2011, another charter crossed the viaduct when GBRf Class 73 Nos 73141 *Charlotte* and 73208 *Kirsten* top-and-tailed the ten-coach 'Mine of Serpents' tour into the by now largely excavated cutting.

Connection and reopening

At around 4pm on 7 March 2013, almost eight years after the excavation of spoil from Imberhorne cutting had begun, the railheads advancing from north and south were finally connected just south of Imberhorne Lane Bridge. A few hours later a GBRf Class 66, running light engine, conducted a gauging run from Tonbridge Yard throughout to Sheffield Park, the first time in almost 50 years that such a route had been physically possible. The following day, 8 March 2013, a 'Golden Spike' ceremony took place under Imberhorne Lane Bridge; the Bluebell Railway's long struggle to reach East Grinstead was complete.

A number of historic 'firsts' followed over the next few days. The first train formation to pass through the cutting operated on 9 March when Class 33 No 33103 *Swordfish*, on hire to the Bluebell, headed north from Sheffield Park hauling an ECS working consisting of a Mark 1 buffet car (destined to become the Bluebell's East Grinstead station buffet) and a brake van. Following this the first steam locomotive over the completed extension was BR Standard Class 9F No 92212, which hauled a test train to East Grinstead, on which many extension

ABOVE The final connection! In lieu of an actual 'golden spike', on 8 March 2013 long-standing Bluebell volunteer Barbara Watkins attaches the ceremonial final fishplate in the northern extension beneath Imberhorne Lane Bridge. *John Sandys*

ABOVE 23 March 2013 – reopening day!
Ex-LBSCR 'E4' Class 0-6-2T No 473 passes
the site of the former Ketches Farm Halt,
just north of Sheffield Park, with 'The Pioneer',
the very first public departure from East
Grinstead to run through to Sheffield Park
in more than five decades. 'P' Class No 323
Bluebell assists at the rear of the train.
Len Walton

RIGHT GBRf Class 66 No 66739 arrives into
Horsted Keynes on 28 March 2013 with the
historic first through railtour from London
since the reconnection with the national
network. *John Sandys*

volunteers rode, on 16 March 2013. Test trains now continued to operate over the coming days before on 23 March 2013, in decidedly wintery weather, the extension was finally opened to the public and the 9.45am departure from Sheffield Park, headed by 1960s stalwarts *Stepney*, *Bluebell* and *Birch Grove*, became the first ever timetabled Bluebell passenger service into East Grinstead. It was four decades since a northern extension had first been mooted in the early 1970s, but the Bluebell Railway had overcome at times seemingly impossible obstacles to achieve its goal. East Grinstead had been reached!

One final historic first was achieved on 28 March 2013 with the operation of the first through railtour from the national network to Sheffield Park since 1963 – indeed, the first through service from London to operate over the northern section of the LEGR since the 1950s. Departing from London Bridge behind GBRf Class 66 No 66739, the formation consisted of 12 coaches and Class 73 Nos 73119 and 73207 on the rear to provide no doubt much-needed train heat. At Horsted Keynes the Class 66 became the third modern traction locomotive to receive the name *Bluebell Railway* – an entirely appropriate choice after the class had played such a large part in the clearing of Imberhorne cutting.

On Sunday 7 April 2013 a Service of Thanksgiving for the completed extension was held at St Swithun's Church, East Grinstead. Addressing the congregation, Bishop Alan Chesters announced, 'The Bluebell Railway has done it and we rejoice!'[59]

ABOVE A close-up of the nameplate of No 66739 *Bluebell Railway*. The Latin motto 'Floreat Vapor' on the Bluebell's crest means, of course, 'Steam shall Flourish'! *John Sandys*

BELOW A picture that says it all, showing the ground frame at East Grinstead, and beyond it the way south across the viaduct is clear ahead to Kingscote, Horsted Keynes and Sheffield Park. Photographed on 30 March 2016, the line to the left of the photographer emerges from the Bluebell platform, while that to the right connects directly to the national network. *Martin Lawrence*

CHAPTER TEN

· · · · · · · · · · · · · · · · · · ·

The Bluebell today – and tomorrow

The Bluebell Railway of today has in some ways changed greatly from
the 4½-mile line that opened in August 1960 with just two tank engines, two
carriages and barely two stations to call its own. The railway now has a running line
of approximately 11 miles, four stations, a connection to the national network and
a fleet of around 30 locomotives, 70 carriages and many historic wagons.

ABOVE Maunsell 'S15' Class No 847 arrives at 'Downton' station (aka Horsted Keynes) with the 11.00am service from Sheffield Park during filming of the *Downton Abbey* TV Christmas special on 5 June 2014. *John Sandys*

LEFT SECR 'C' Class No 592 approaches Kingscote with an up 'Golden Arrow' dining service on 30 May 2010. The structure on the right is the temporary signal cabin that controlled movements at Kingscote from reopening until early 2016. The Bluebell prides itself on the authenticity of its regular Pullman dining services – even to the extent of insisting on a 'smart' dress code for Pullman passengers! At present four vintage Pullman cars are available for service, but a fifth is to be restored with the help of a £75,000 Department for Transport grant. As part of its restoration, Parlour Brake Car No 54 will be made fully wheelchair accessible, allowing passengers of restricted mobility full access to the Pullman dining experience. *Martin Lawrence*

One of the largest tourist attractions in Sussex, the line is regularly seen by millions of viewers in countless film and TV appearances (most notably of late, Horsted Keynes has been seen as 'Downton' station in Downton Abbey) and was recently described by *The Railway Magazine* as being in the 'Premier League' of UK heritage railways.[60] But for all the changes that have occurred over the course of more than five and a half decades, the pioneering spirit, ambition and unique atmosphere

of the Bluebell continues to this day, with major new developments and improvements either already under way or planned for the future.

Rolling stock

Although the Bluebell of today exists in a world in which heritage railways sometimes seem to be two-a-penny, it is perhaps its rolling stock more than anything else that continues to set it apart from many of its competitors. Aside from a couple of diesel shunters and the occasional advertised 'Diesel Days' (of which more below). the Bluebell remains an entirely steam-operated railway and, true to the aims of its 1960s pioneers, is almost entirely dominated by classes that would once have been common in the south-east of England. The railway's locomotive fleet is one of the finest outside the National Railway Museum and can boast the UK's largest collection of engines from the Southern Railway and its predecessors (including no fewer than five engines owned by the Maunsell Locomotive Society and two owned by the Bulleid Society), as well as the largest collection of BR Standard locomotives. At any one time around eight locomotives are usually operational (it is not uncommon to see four locomotives in steam on a two-train operating day), with around four undergoing overhaul and the rest of the collection mostly on display at Sheffield Park.

TOP LEFT Ex-SECR 'P' Class No 323 *Bluebell* passes south through Kingscote's reconstructed Platform 2 with a rake of restored historic goods wagons on 19 March 2016. *Martin Lawrence*

BOTTOM LEFT Ex-SECR 'C' Class No 592 approaches the southern portal of Sharpthorne Tunnel – the longest tunnel on any UK heritage railway – on 6 September 2015. *Martin Lawrence*

ABOVE Seen here at Kingscote on 7 March 2015, 1877-built Fletcher Jennings 0-4-0T *Captain Baxter* (aka *Baxter*) was actually one of the first locomotives to arrive on the Bluebell Railway in 1960, but, save for a single steaming, was not returned to service until 1982. Although too small to work regular service trains, *Baxter* is often employed as a station pilot at Sheffield Park and, since 2010, has been fitted with vacuum brakes, enabling it to work occasional light passenger trains. *Keith Duke*

The Bluebell's fleet of around 70 carriages is no less impressive or historic, with only a minority representing the BR Mark 1s that often dominate on other heritage railways. Around 30 carriages are usually available for service, including ex-Southern Railway Maunsell and Bulleid designs, Pullman coaches dating from the 1920s and around a dozen pre-Grouping carriages, some restored from grounded coach bodies. Many more are awaiting restoration.

Diesel galas and visiting locomotives

The Bluebell has long played host to visiting locomotives, but since the completion of the northern extension the appearance of 'foreign' engines at Sheffield Park has become a more frequent occurrence. One such loco to arrive via the main-line link at East Grinstead is celebrity 'new-build' LNER-design Peppercorn 'A1' Class No 60163 *Tornado*, which in September 2013 hauled the first steam-hauled railtour to run from London to Sheffield Park for 50 years.

The ease with which locomotives can now visit the Bluebell has led to another innovation, already common on many heritage lines: diesel galas. Since the once resolutely steam-only Bluebell Railway has no diesel fleet of its own (save for the presence of a couple of shunters, themselves a fairly recent addition to the railway's stock list), such events were previously out of the question, but since 2014 have gradually started to appear on the Bluebell's calendar. Not

WHISTLE

ABOVE An East Coast diesel thoroughbred might be unexpected on a railway normally devoted to preserving Southern steam, but there's no doubt that No 55019 *Royal Highland Fusilier* makes an imposing site as it bursts from the north portal of Sharpthorne Tunnel on 18 April 2015 during the Bluebell's highly successful 'Deltic weekend'. *Keith Duke*

TOP LEFT Visiting new-build Peppercorn 'A1' 'Pacific' No 60163 *Tornado* passes the site of West Hoathly station with the 12.15pm departure from Sheffield Park on 28 July 2014. *John Sandys*

BOTTOM LEFT An unusual line-up at Sheffield Park on 14 April 2016: Class 73 electro-diesels Nos 73964 *Jeanette*, 73136 *Mhairi* and 73119 *Borough of Eastleigh* pose outside the engine shed during the 2016 diesel gala. To the right can be seen the frames of Southern Railway 'Schools' Class No 928 *Stowe*. *Len Walton*

surprisingly, the appearance of so-called modern traction on a railway whose founding purpose was to 'preserve the puffer for posterity' was controversial, but the undoubted success of the events, such as a multi-engine GBRf gala in April 2016, has quickly won over many critics. A 2015 'Deltic' Gala prompted the Editor of *The Railway Magazine* to write:

'Society changes to reflect the tastes of each succeeding generation and I therefore have to admit that the huge crowds boosting the Bluebell's coffers when two "Deltics" took over the line in April have made me think again. As long as such events are kept in moderation, they might be a good thing after all.'[61]

New-build locomotives

In October 2000, having acquired a suitable boiler, the Bluebell became one of the first heritage groups to announce its aim to construct a replica 'new-build' example of a long-lost locomotive type. In this case the loco was No 32424 *Beachy Head*, the last surviving Brighton 'Atlantic', which was sadly scrapped in 1958, just a few months before the Bluebell Railway Preservation Society was founded. With work on the 'Atlantic' now entering its final stages, the hope is that *Beachy Head* will take to the rails in 2018, 60 years after its namesake was lost.

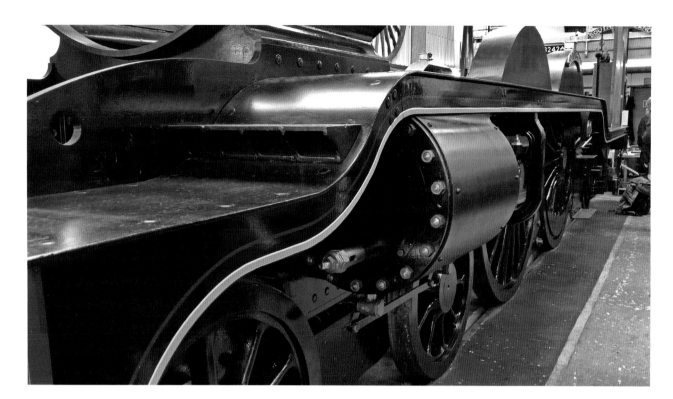

With the Bluebell's Long Term Plan, published in 2013, including a commitment to 'construct replicas of locomotives which are particularly appropriate to the collection, and to the operation of the Railway'[62], work on a second partial new-build is also now under way, with BR Standard Class 2MT 2-6-0 tender locomotive No 78059 being converted into BR Standard Class 2MT 2-6-2T No 84030 – another class that was lost to posterity. With the Long Term Plan also promising to 'Commence construction of a replica LB&SCR "Craven era" locomotive'[63] within the next ten years, it seems that *Beachy Head* and the Standard Class 2 tank will not be the last new-builds to emerge from the works at Sheffield Park.

'Operation Undercover'

As early as 1970 the Bluebell set about raising funds to store some of its historic, and at that stage rapidly decaying, carriage fleet undercover, and in January 1971 a four-track shed was constructed on the former goods yard site at Horsted Keynes. A locomotive works was constructed at Sheffield Park in the 1970s, meaning that major overhauls could be undertaken undercover without being contracted out, followed in the 1980s by a new locomotive shed, replacing the primitive facilities built in the railway's earliest years.

At the dawn of the new millennium the Bluebell launched 'Operation Undercover', an ongoing project to create covered accommodation for the protection and restoration of its priceless collection of vehicles. Under this banner the early years of the century saw the existing Horsted Keynes carriage shed refurbished and externally re-clad in a Southern Railway

ABOVE A close-up of the driving wheels and frames of 'new-build' Brighton 'Atlantic' No 32424 *Beachy Head*. Seen here on 13 June 2015, it is hoped that the loco will enter service on the Bluebell in 2018. *Martin Lawrence*

TOP RIGHT The changing face of Sheffield Park station in the 21st century, viewed from the footbridge installed in 1985. The main building on Platform 1 is largely unchanged since the 1880s (a modern restaurant, shop and offices are all out of shot on the extreme right), but much development can be seen on Platform 2. The small structure nearest the camera is the Bulleid Society shop, while beyond it the extended former waiting room houses the Bluebell's museum. In front of the museum, the platform canopy has been restored to its original length while behind can be seen the carriage storage shed completed in 2011. In the platform stands the ex-Metropolitan Railway 'Chesham' set. *John Sandys*

BOTTOM RIGHT Construction of 'Operation Undercover' phase 4, involving a major extension to the existing carriage facilities at Horsted Keynes, is well under way in this view from 17 May 2016. In the foreground stands newly restored SECR Full 3rd No 3188, which re-entered service in June 2016. *John Sandys*

style, and the locomotive shed at Sheffield Park extended. Following this, Phase 3 of 'Operation Undercover' saw construction begin in 2009 of a new carriage storage facility at Sheffield Park, capable of providing covered accommodation for up to 17 vehicles. Completed in 2011, this phase also included the construction of a major new museum, the

ABOVE BR Standard Class 5MT No 73082 *Camelot* returned to service after a 10-year overhaul in October 2015, and is seen here in 2016 approaching Hill Place Bridge with a northbound service through the former tip site at Imberhorne cutting. With the northern extension complete, the Bluebell's ambitions are now turning westward, with the Ardingly branch seriously on the agenda. *Len Walton*

restoration of the canopy on Platform 2 to its original length, and a new locomotive washout pit.

With yet more covered accommodation required to protect as much as possible of the Bluebell's historic carriage fleet from the elements, the latest phase of 'Operation Undercover', ongoing at the time of writing, involves the construction of a major extension to the existing Carriage & Wagon Works at Horsted Keynes, capable of holding approximately 20 further vehicles. Depending on the availability of funding, thoughts are now turning towards future redevelopment of the locomotive facilities at Sheffield Park – including the possible conversion of the existing engine shed into an accessible modern exhibition area.

Bluebell Railway Museum

The Bluebell's museum, part of the Bluebell Railway Trust, holds Accredited Museum status and as mentioned above was greatly expanded by the construction of a new building in 2011. Part funded by a grant from the Heritage Lottery Fund,

the new structure stands on the up platform at Sheffield Park. Future aims include the creation of a Research and Records Centre to house an archive of material from across the Southern Railway and its constituent companies.

West Hoathly and the Ardingly branch

Proposals laid out for the next ten years in the Bluebell's Long Term Plan include the hope of establishing a station at West Hoathly and also working towards the relaying of the Ardingly branch. For the West Hoathly site the proposal is possibly to begin with a low-key halt with the ultimate intention of building an LBSCR-style station, 'sympathetic to the architectural appearance of other Bluebell stations'[64].

The proposed reinstatement of the Ardingly branch, mentioned in Chapter Two, will arguably be the biggest challenge for the Bluebell since the reconstruction of the line to East Grinstead. The trackbed from Horsted Keynes to Ardingly was bought by the railway as far back as 1997, and in October 2013 the Bluebell took delivery of two redundant bridge spans, formerly used to carry the Malvern to Ashchurch line over the M50, which will be used to replace the missing Sheriff Mill Viaduct, demolished in 1968. No firm date has been set for the project, with any physical reconstruction unlikely to take place until funds are available and a backlog of routine maintenance between Sheffield Park and Horsted Keynes has been dealt with, but already a protected route through the stone terminal that occupies the Ardingly station site has been agreed. Beyond Ardingly, the line towards Haywards Heath remains in Network Rail ownership and continues to serve the stone terminal, but the Bluebell is still hopeful of negotiating running rights over this section. In 2014 it was announced that a site for a new Bluebell station had been reserved in Haywards Heath, with *The Railway Magazine* reporting that 'The local authority ensured land was safeguarded for the future provision of a Bluebell Railway platform by making it a condition of the planning permission granted for the Haywards Heath station redevelopment.'[65] As at East Grinstead, the Bluebell's proposed new station is again to stand between the Network Rail station and a supermarket development!

Laid out under the heading 'Projects aspired to for the 25 year period to 2038' in the Bluebell's Long Term Plan is the proposal to consider electrifying the Ardingly branch[66], meaning that the once determinedly steam-only Bluebell might one day become the first heritage line on which preserved third-rail

BELOW Ex-LBSCR 'E4' Class No 32494 departs from Lewes with a 9.30am service for East Grinstead in October 1956, not long after the short-lived revival of the route. It may seem impossible to imagine that steam trains will ever depart this way for East Grinstead again, but the Bluebell Railway has never been afraid to dream the impossible.
Bluebell Railway Museum Archive

EMUs can operate under their own power! Which units might be available to operate over the Ardingly branch remains to be seen, but no doubt the Bluebell's own preserved 4-VEP No 3417 *Gordon Pettitt* would be among them.

Extending south?

With East Grinstead reached and the Ardingly branch being actively considered, the only other direction for the Bluebell to go is south. In practice this would be a much tougher project to tackle; the realigned A275 road immediately south of Sheffield Park would need to be overcome and, more significantly, the route through Newick & Chailey is blocked by the housing estate built over the infilled cutting where the station once stood. Nonetheless the Bluebell's aspirations for the next quarter-century include the intention to investigate 'a southerly extension to Lewes via Newick and Chailey and Barcombe'. If this should ever come to fruition it would mean that the Bluebell Railway had succeeded in restoring the entire LEGR network constructed in the years 1878-83. Indeed, south of Culver Junction (physically the southernmost limit of the old LEGR) the Bluebell would also have to reconstruct part of the Uckfield-Lewes line, closed in 1969, if it were ever to reach Lewes itself.

Whatever happens, it seems that the Lewes & East Grinstead Railway, built in the 19th century and closed twice in the 1950s, will continue to have an exciting future in the 21st century.

Notes

Chapter 1

1 *The Times*, 'Railway and Other Companies' (20 November 1876), p7
2 Frederick McDermott, quoted in Klaus Marx, *An Illustrated History of the Lewes & East Grinstead Railway* (2000), p25
3 Quoted in Klaus Marx, op cit, p26
4 Ibid, p64

Chapter 2

5 Klaus Marx, *An Illustrated History of the Lewes & East Grinstead Railway* (2000), p60
6 Note that all references to 'BR' in this book refer to British Railways, not the Bluebell Railway!
7 Quoted in Klaus Marx, op cit, p65
8 *The Railway Magazine*, 'The Lewes and East Grinstead Railway' (October 1954), p671

Chapter 3

9 *The Railway Magazine*, 'The Lewes and East Grinstead Railway' (October 1954), p672

Chapter 5

10 *Sussex Express & County Herald*, 'The Future of East Sussex Railways' (11 December 1953), p6
11 *Sussex Express & County Herald*, 'Closure of Lewes to East Grinstead Rail Line Recommended' (7 May 1954), p3
12 *Sussex Express & County Herald*, 'More Buses If Trains Are Withdrawn' (11 June 1954), p3
13 *Sussex Express & County Herald*, 'Drop Closure Proposals, Improve Services' (18 June 1954), p8
14 *Sussex Express & County Herald*, 'Barcombe Call For More Trains, Not Extra Buses' (6 August 1954), p7
15 *Sussex Express & County Herald*, 'Fletching Call For Adequate Bus Alternative' (18 June 1954), p8
16 *Sussex Express & County Herald*, 'Villagers Answer Transport Chief' (9 July 1954), p3
17 *Sussex Express & County Herald*, 'Rail Closing Not Foregone Conclusion' (5 November 1954), p3
18 *Sussex Express & County Herald*, 'Another Nail In The Coffin Of A Branch Line' (3 December 1954), p9

Chapter 6

19 *The Illustrated London News*, '"Ice" in August; Naval and Railway News; and the Eisteddfod' (18 August 1956), p257
20 Quoted in Klaus Marx, *An Illustrated History of the Lewes & East Grinstead Railway* (2000), p223

21 *The Times*, 'Newhaven-Dieppe Winter Closing Supported' (14 August 1959), p7
22 *The Manchester Guardian*, 'Branch Line to Reopen?' (28 April 1956), p6
23 *The Manchester Guardian*, 'Victory Uncertain' (13 June 1956), p6
24 *Sussex Express & County Herald*, 'Barcombe Has Best Kept Cricket Ground' (5 November 1954), p7
25 Klaus Marx, *An Illustrated History of the Lewes & East Grinstead Railway* (2000), p223
26 *The Railway Magazine*, 'The Lewes and East Grinstead Railway' (October 1954), pp665-73

Chapter 7

27 *The Manchester Guardian*, 'Closure of the "Bluebell Line"' (13 February 1958), p8
28 Quoted in Klaus Marx, *An Illustrated History of the Lewes & East Grinstead Railway* (2000), pp234-35
29 *The Times*, '"Bluebell Line" to Close in March' (13 February 1958), p3
30 *The Times*, 'Last Train on the "Bluebell Line"' (17 March 1958), p5
31 *The Washington Post and Times Herald*, '1882 Bluebell & Primrose Bows Out, Its Snail's Pace at Last Too Slow' (17 March 1958)
32 *The Times*, 'Personal' (18 March 1959), p1
33 Any goodwill from Miss Bessemer towards the preservationists seems to have been sadly short-lived. A letter in the Bluebell Railway archives reveals that little over a year later, in April 1960, she was writing to the Bluebell's own Captain Peter Manisty to complain of an interview he had given to Good Housekeeping magazine: 'On what authority did you state that I had "left off"? What aspect of my work has been carried on … by your Society? … What is the "better victory" your Society have won?'
34 *The Manchester Guardian*, 'The "Bluebell Line" – Society hoping to reopen it' (16 March 1959), p1
35 *The Times*, 'Plan to Buy Part of "Bluebell Line"' (15 June 1959), p6
36 *The Manchester Guardian*, 'Take-over in Sussex: Bluebell Line' (28 September 1959), p5
37 *The Times*, 'Bluebell Line Sale – Society Hope to Take Over in May' (28 September 1959), p8
38 *The Times*, '"Bluebell" Line Needs £2,250 A Year' (20 February 1960), p4
39 *The Times*, 'Company To Run The Bluebell Line' (25 February 1960), p3

40 *The Guardian*, 'Railway Society Buys Its First Engine' (9 May 1960), p4

41 *The Observer*, 'Crucial Day for Bluebell Railway' (10 July 1960), p9

42 *The Baltimore Sun*, 'England's 4½-Mile Rail Line Reopens' (8 August 1960), p3

Chapter 8

43 *The Times*, '12,000 Travelled on Bluebell Line' (25 October 1960), p12

44 *The Times*, 'Bluebell Line Shows a Healthy Profit' (5 December 1960), p5

45 T. C. Cole, *Guidebook to the Bluebell Railway* (1966), p22

46 T. C. Cole, *Steaming On!* (1970), p13

47 T. C. Cole, *Guidebook to the Bluebell Railway* (1966), p8

48 *The Railway Magazine*, 'GWR 4-4-0 Preservation Fund' (December 1960), p884

49 T. C. Cole, *Guidebook to the Bluebell Railway* (1966), p7

Chapter 9

50 Quoted in *Railway World Special: The Bluebell Railway* (1988), p17

51 *The Railway Magazine*, 'Bluebell Aims North' (February 1976), pp60-63

52 *The Times*, 'Bluebell line to link with British Rail' (6 April 1985), p3

53 *The Guardian*, 'Bluebell to grow' (25 November 1985), p2

54 *Bluebell Railway PLC 1986 Share Issue* (1986), p8

55 *The Times*, 'Minister toasts railway' (14 March 1988), p2

56 *The Guardian*, 'Bluebell issue' (13 February 1991), p14

57 *The Railway Magazine*, 'Bluebell ready to sign Imberhorne agreement' (August 2007), p62

58 Colin Tyson (ed), *Battle for Bluebell* (2013), p79

59 Ibid, p126

Chapter 10

60 *The Railway Magazine*, 'The Heritage Railway "Premier League", 2015' (June 2015), p21

61 *The Railway Magazine*, 'Has the Bluebell got it right after all?' (May 2015), p3

62 Objectives, Aims & Plans of the Bluebell Railway Preservation Society (2013), p10

63 Ibid, p14

64 Ibid, p8

65 *The Railway Magazine*, 'Site for Bluebell station in Haywards Heath safeguarded' (April 2014), p66

66 *Objectives, Aims & Plans of the Bluebell Railway Preservation Society* (2013), p14

Bibliography

Battle for Bluebell by C. Tyson (ed) (Mortons Media Group, 2013)

Bluebell News (Bluebell Railway, various issues 2014-16)

The Bluebell Railway: A Past and Present Companion by T. Gough (Past & Present Publishing, 1998)

The Bluebell Railway: Five Decades of Achievement by M. Welch (Capital Transport, 2010)

Bluebell Railway PLC: 1986 Share Issue (Bluebell Railway, 1986)

Bluebell Railway PLC: 1991 Share Issue (Bluebell Railway, 1991)

Bluebell Railway: Steaming On! by T. C. Cole (Bluebell Railway, 1970)

Bluebell Railway Recollections by K. Leppard (Silver Link Publishing, 2013)

Guidebook to the Bluebell Railway by T. C. Cole (Bluebell Railway, 1966)

An Illustrated History of the Lewes & East Grinstead Railway by K. Marx (Oxford Publishing Co, 2000)

'The Lewes & East Grinstead Railway' by R. C. Riley (*The Railway Magazine*, October 1954, pp665-73)

Portrait of Bluebell Steam by M. Welch (Runpast Publishing, 1997)

Rails to Sheffield Park by M. Welch (Kingfisher Railway Productions, 1988)

Railway World Special: The Bluebell Railway (Ian Allan, 1988)

Target East Grinstead: Bluebell Railway PLC Offer for Sale of Shares (Bluebell Railway, 2008)

Vintage Bluebell: The Early Years in Colour by M. Welch (Runpast Publishing, 2005)

Online resources

Bluebell Railway www.bluebellrailway.co.uk

Disused Stations www.disused-stations.org.uk

Find My Past: British Newspapers www.findmypast.co.uk/search/british-newspapers

ProQuest Historical Newspapers www.proquest.com/products-services/pq-hist-news.html

Railway Magazine Digital Archive www.railwaymagazine.co.uk/archive

The Times Digital Archive www.gale.cengage.co.uk/times.aspx

Index